UNDERACHIEVEMENT: REVERSING THE PROCESS

A parents guide for assisting
your underachiever to success

Carolyn Warnemuende, M.S.
John H. Samson, M.D.

FAMILY LIFE
PUBLICATIONS
Sunset Beach, California

Manufactured in the United States of America

The authors of this book have provided information to help you cooperate with your physician, mental health, and educational professionals in mutually guiding your underachieving child toward success. They are dispensing neither medical nor psychological advice. The authors and publisher assume no responsibility or liability for any actions, or for the results of those actions, which you may take as a result of the information herein contained.

ISBN 0-9628925-1-3
Library of Congress Catalog Card Number 91-70386

Cover by Pam Adams

Contents

8 The Child with a Learning Disability   106

What Is a Learning Disability? • Who Are the
Learning-disabled? • What Causes Learning
Disabilities? • Common Behavior Patterns
of Children with a Learning Disability • How
the Child Copes with His Learning Disability •
Social Patterns of Learning-disabled Children •
Diagnosis of the Learning-disabled • Remediation
for the Learning-disabled • Academic Remediation •
Social and Emotional Remediation in the School •
Social and Emotional Remediation in the Home •
What Can I Expect for the Future? • Check List
for Learning Disability • Check List for Evaluation
of Services

9 The Child with an Emotional
Disorder   134

What Is an Emotional Disorder? • The Role of
the Family with the Emotionally Disturbed
Child • The Overly Anxious Child • Intervention
for the Overly Anxious Child • Parenting the
Overly Anxious Child • The Oppositional Child •
Intervention for the Oppositional Child •
Parenting the Oppositional Child • The Child
with Adjustment Problems • Intervention for
the Child with Adjustment Problems • Parenting
the Child with Adjustment Problems • The
Adolescent with an Identity Disorder •
Intervention for the Adolescent with an
Identity Disorder • Parenting the Troubled
Teen • Check List for Emotional Disorders •
Check List for Evaluation of Services

10 The Child Who Is a Slow Learner   163

Who Is the Slow Learner? • What Causes Low IQ? • Characteristics of the Slow Learner • Remediation for the Slow Learner • Academic Remediation • Support in the Home • What About the Future? • Check List for the Slow Learner • Check List for Evaluation of Services

11 The Power of Success   183

I've Done This Before • Let Me Think About It • I Really Want To, and I Just Can't • The Power of Success

Index   195

Acknowledgments

With joy and pleasure we offer thanks to all those who helped bring this book into being:

Our families for their love, support, and assistance.

Our friends for their encouragement and interest.

Our patients and clients who provided the opportunity for us to develop the process for releasing the power of success in underachieving students.

The parents and professionals who willingly offered ideas and feedback during the preparation of the manuscript—Karyl Ann Armbruster, M.A.; Michele Blair, M.S.; Molly Debysingh, Ph.D.; Kay Kaplan; Nancy Levin; Nancy Linden, M.S.; Philip F. Newberg, Ph.D.; David H. Payne, M.D.; Margaret Payne; Vivian Philippi; Carol Samson; Sandi Capuano Smith, Ph.D.; Virginia Sponsler, M.S.W; Barbara Springosky; Jacky Trani; and M. James Warnemuende, Ph.D.

And to Pam Adams for her assistance with design and for creating the cover, Gladys Carlson for her generosity and meticulousness in editing, Todd Paddock for his dauntlessness and expertise in publishing, and Thomas Sponsler, J.D. for his legal advice.

To the Reader

Since we are not talking to each of you individually about your child, we had to make a decision about the use of the pronouns *he* and *she*. More males than females are academic underachievers, so we use the pronoun *he* when referring to the underachiever. *He* is also used to designate the physician since medicine continues to be a male-dominated profession. All educational and mental health professionals are referred to as *she*. Many men are teachers, diagnosticians, and mental health workers; however, those specializing in work with children are most often women.

1

An Introduction to the Problem

This is a book about a serious educational problem. It is also a book about love, the love of parents for their children. It is about loving and assisting children who make up a large percentage of the students in our schools—underachievers. In the United States, as many as one out of four students functions a year and a half or more below grade level, and the numbers are rising. Millions of children sit in classrooms working below their potential. These children need special assistance to release their power for success. As a loving parent, you are the primary catalyst in this process.

A loving parent must have more than a feeling of affection for his or her child. Parental love requires effectively guiding our children toward success. It is not always easy to love our children when they do not turn out the way we thought or hoped they would. It is impossible to love when we feel afraid or incompetent. If our child is not doing well in school, often we do not know what to do. We feel helpless and inadequate because we do not know what steps to take to assist him. These feelings reflect in our interactions with our children. We put pressure on them and react angrily or with impatience to their lack of success. Our love is buried beneath our fears and cannot be felt by our offspring.

This book suggests definite steps to take when your son or daughter is not a successful student. Through gaining knowledge you will gain confidence and competence. You will be able to assist your child with understanding and love. No one can motivate another person. Motivation has to come from inside one's self. We can inspire motivation in another, however. When parents know the steps to take to assist their underachieving child with love, there is the likelihood of inspiring the desire for success in the youngster. Children do not know how to help themselves when they are not achieving in school. They need guidance. They need someone to assist them in releasing the power for success which is inherently inside of them. You can do this!

Imagine that your employer assigns you to a job for which you are untrained, and you will not receive on-the-job training. You are told it is the most important job you will ever undertake. It is a task which demands responsibility and requires expert communication skills, patience, flexibility, understanding, self-control, and creativity.

"I could never do something like that," you are thinking. "It would be impossible." No, not impossible. You already have such a job. You accepted these very responsibilities when you became a parent.

Think a minute about parenthood. Whether you planned to have a child, "accidentally" had a baby, slipped into parenthood because it was the next stage in your life, or adopted a child, you expected you would be successful. Oh, you knew there would be some rough spots, but, overall, your expectations were for success.

To make sure you knew whether you and your infant were on target, perhaps you read books to better understand growth and development. More than likely Dr. Spock helped you determine when your baby or young child needed a doctor. You made regular well-check visits to the pediatrician. If your toddler attended preschool, there were parent meetings where you learned discipline strategies, how to enrich your home environment, and how to know when he was ready for kindergarten.

These kinds of support are necessary for parents. It feels good when you recognize that you are on the right track. It is comforting to have guidance when you are not.

Often, after a child leaves preschool, the educational system becomes less supportive for parents. If your child is succeeding in school, you may have contact with the teacher only at parent conference time. If he is not succeeding, you probably are apprised regularly of the situation; however, in many instances, you are not given the guidance or support necessary to assist him toward success.

When your child grows emotionally, socially, and academically in a way that meets your and society's expectations, you feel competent and successful in your parenting. When he does not, you feel ineffective and as if somehow you have failed. If you are like most parents, you also feel guilty. You think you should know what to do when your youngster is having problems. You forget you have never been trained to parent in the best of times, let alone when problems arise that even experts do not agree on how to handle.

In *Underachievement: Reversing the Process,* the authors give you the on-the-job training you need to guide your youngster toward success. It is the result of 25 years of successful work with children who do and do not do well as students. Independently and together we have educated, doctored, and counseled children who learn and do not learn and parents who are and are not effective. Through our work together, we developed a system for identifying, diagnosing, and treating children who do not achieve as well in school as they could. During the past 10 years, this approach has brought success to hundreds of children and families. We now share this approach with you.

As well as being professionals, we are parents. Between our two individual families, we have raised and are still parenting 15 children who currently range in age from 10 to 29 years. Like you, we have each experienced the joys and frustrations, the pain and occasional guilt associated with parenthood. We and our spouses have learned from our experiences to parent positively and effectively. In each chapter we provide parenting techniques which we have found effective in our families and professional practices which we know will be valuable in your family, too.

Assisting your child toward success requires 10 steps:
1. Recognize that a problem exists
2. Discuss your concerns with your child's physician
3. Have the appropriate evaluations
4. Follow through with the recommendations provided
5. Be an effective consumer of professional services
6. Ask for what you are not getting
7. Increase your repertoire of parenting skills
8. Use your parenting skills consistently
9. Create experiences where your child can succeed
10. Acknowledge each step toward success

Each of these steps is necessary for optimal success in all children who are not succeeding in school. Our purpose is to show you how to use the steps and support you in your efforts to assist your youngster by relaying the information in such a way that your questions about underachievement are answered. When you know what underachievement is and what to do about it, you will feel competent about taking the steps to help your child.

If you are concerned about your child's level of achievement, you are filled with many questions. How do I know if he is doing as well as he should? Why isn't he learning better? Can't the school do something? What should I do? Why doesn't he seem to care? Why does he worry so much? We answer all of these questions and more. Chapter by chapter we take you through the 10-step process necessary in determining whether your child is underachieving and what to do about it.

Underachievement currently receives wide media coverage. Television specials and magazine articles inform you about the syndrome. Advertisements alerting you to clinics and programs to assist underachievers abound. The plight of these youngsters is being confronted as an educational issue which needs addressing.

Each day hundreds of parents like you seek the advice and counsel of physicians, mental health workers, and learning specialists. Only a fortunate few of the families receive effective guidance and treatment. The rest become shoppers, frantically searching for answers to the problem or resigning themselves to the dilemma in the belief that there is no answer.

Why don't underachievers and their families receive the help they need? Until recently, underachievement was viewed as a diagnosis, as the problem itself, rather than a symptom or sign of a problem. Therapy designed to remediate underachievement failed because the underlying condition was not treated.

The symptom of underachievement can be compared to the physical symptoms of coughing or vomiting. When your child exhibits these symptoms, you know they are signs of an illness. They are not the diagnosis or illness itself. When the physician examines your child and identifies the cause of the coughing or vomiting, he can prescribe the appropriate treatment.

Perhaps you cannot get to a doctor immediately, so you give your child a cough drop to calm his cough or warm tea to settle his stomach. The symptoms may subside temporarily but will return until the correct diagnosis and treatment provide long-lasting effects.

What if you ignore the symptoms? If the coughing or vomiting is the result of a simple cold or case of the flu, your child may experience increased discomfort and the symptoms may last longer, but he will usually get well. Ignoring the symptoms, however, may increase the severity of the illness or leave a more serious disorder undetected.

Unfortunately, underachievement is not as easily remedied as most medical illnesses. Temporary measures are no more effective than a cough drop or hot tea. The only way to achieve effective results with under-achievement is to correctly diagnose the underlying cause and follow the specific prescribed treatment. The underlying causes are: attention deficit disorder with hyperactivity, attention deficit disorder without hyperactiv-ity, learning disability, emotional disorders, low IQ, and certain medical problems.

Ignoring underachievement never improves the situation. The longer the underachiever goes undiagnosed, the greater the academic, social, and emotional problems he faces. His lack of success results in poor self-esteem and diminished motivation. In short, he does not feel good about himself.

Without help, children and adolescents who do not feel good about themselves grow into adults with feelings of low self-worth. When people do not feel worthy they are not fully effective in relationships or chosen careers and activities. Treating the underachiever is mandatory if he is to attain a fulfilling life.

Assisting the underachiever requires a team approach. The child, parent, physician, learning specialist, mental health worker, and classroom teacher are the members of the team. Each plays a vital role in the process of guiding the underachiever toward success.

As a member of the team, it is imperative that you be knowledgeable. You must know how to be an effective advocate and consumer of services for your child. You must have understanding so that you can provide the effective parenting he needs. If you do not know how to ask for and get appropriate help and cannot provide the proper guidance and support in the home, his chances for success are significantly lessened.

In the following pages we provide basic knowledge about underachievement and each of the disorders resulting in the syndrome. Check lists with common characteristics of underachieving children and adolescents are included with each chapter. Information is given about what you can expect from professionals who work with your child. Here, too, check lists provide the opportunity for you to evaluate whether the services he is receiving are adequate. In short, after reading this book, you will know the steps to take to get the best possible help for your underachiever.

Some of you may wonder whether it is necessary to use the check lists. Through our experience, we have discovered that lists such as the ones we have developed assist parents in seeing their child more clearly. They provide a framework for organizing information about the child. This can save valuable time when seeking professional guidance. The lists we have devised are by no means comprehensive. They do not cover all the characteristics exhibited by children. They do, however, cover the most commonly observed traits of children with disorders leading to underachievement.

The check lists designed to assist you in evaluating the services your youngster is receiving are unique. They cover what we believe is essential to you as a consumer of medical, educational, and mental health services. Most lay persons do not know exactly what professionals in the medical, educational, and mental health fields do to assist their clients toward success. Many people feel in awe of these professionals because of their education, expertise, or title. If this is how you feel, it is not comfortable for you to ask questions about your child's progress or lack of progress. Our intent is to provide you with both the knowledge and the tools necessary to become a well-informed, powerful consumer who knows what to ask for and how to get it.

The route suggested is not quick or easy. It is efficient, but requires time and persistence. If it is followed, however, your child will become a more successful student who feels good about himself and his accomplishments. He will function more effectively—academically, socially, and in the family. You will feel better for and about him and be able to express your love for him more fully. The dividends to him, your family, and you cannot be overemphasized.

We have not written a "how to parent" manual in the usual sense. It does not cover a wide range of family situations with solutions to the problems encountered in child rearing. It assists you in solving a very specific problem. The parenting suggestions we have included work well with children exhibiting the disorders leading to underachievement and may not be covered in general parenting books. It takes time for behavior and relationships to change. Patience and a willingness to incorporate these suggestions into your current parenting practices will bring results.

You have taken a big step by picking up this book. You have moved from worry and wondering to action. You have acknowledged to yourself that your child may have a problem and that you are ready to confront that problem by learning more about it. Congratulations! Now we invite you to take the next step and discover how to lovingly release the power for success and ability to learn in this wonderful child of yours.

2

The Underachieving Child

All of us want our children to succeed in life. Most of us believe that a good education provides greater opportunity for success. Whether we use the public school system or send our youngsters to a private school, we know that our children must be active participants in the educational process, or learning will not take place. Active participation depends on a child's ability to concentrate, to effectively process written and spoken language, to stay on task, and on his motivation to achieve.

Most of us expect that our children will succeed as students just as we expect to succeed as parents. When they do not, we are confused, disappointed, angry, and afraid. Whether the lack of success is in academic skills, social behavior, or both, the recognition that our youngster is not doing well causes pain. We hurt for him and for ourselves.

We often express this hurt by blaming the child, the school, or our own choices of action or inaction. We nag our son or daughter about homework and tests. We say things like, "If you'd just try harder, you'd do better." We remember all the things we have not liked about the school system and all the teachers who, we felt, did not do their best job. "This is the third year in a row he's had a bad teacher," we complain. We berate ourselves by recalling events from pregnancy, birth, and early childhood that we fear contributed to the problem. "I knew I shouldn't have played tennis throughout my pregnancy. Probably all the jostling around did something to his brain," we lament.

Blame, fear, and regret do not help the child. They create stress within the family and keep parents immobilized. If our child is not doing well in school, we must put our hurt and disappointment aside and do what must be done to help our youngster back onto the track of success.

What Is Underachievement?

The first step in handling a problem is to carefully define it. Clarity about what we are facing often points the way to an effective solution. The problem of underachievement is not easily defined because it has different meanings to professionals in different occupations. This is one of the reasons many underachievers do not receive the help they need. Vague definitions of problems lead to vague, ineffective solutions.

Underachievement is commonly used as an umbrella term to describe anyone who is not performing in a particular activity as well as someone who knows that activity well thinks he should. Usually the term refers to lack of academic success; however, adults who choose jobs that do not reflect the degrees they hold or athletes who fail to perform to their potential could also be referred to as underachievers.

Academic underachievement is what is likely to send you running to the pediatrician, mental health worker, or learning specialist for help. In the past, there has been little consistency in the selection and labeling of academic underachievers. Some experts have used the label only for intellectually superior students whose academic performance is dramatically below that level. Others have used the term for students functioning a year and a half or more below grade level. Teachers have used the word to describe students who are not keeping up in class. Parents have said their child is underachieving if he is not making the grades they want him to make or that a sibling has attained.

Since we know the first step in seeking a solution to a problem is creating a clear definition, academic underachievement must be defined by you and all professionals working with you and your youngster in the same way. The definition of academic underachievement we use is short and concise. It is comprehensive and can be applied to any student regardless of his age or intellectual ability. It is measurable. Students, parents, and professionals can objectively see change and steps toward success.

Academic underachievement means that your child's performance in academic subjects is below an expected level as indicated by his measured abilities on intelligence and aptitude tests. Although we call the child an underachiever, remember, underachievement is not a diagnosis. It is not the primary problem. It is a symptom or sign that there is a problem which .

results in underachievement. It is an indication that some underlying cause is preventing the child from expressing all that he knows. There is something happening in his body, his thought processes, or his emotional life which interferes with his success as a student.

Any student, whether male or female, gifted or slow learner, can be an underachiever. Underachievement cannot be guessed at, however. Individually administered intelligence and achievement tests must be used to determine whether a child is working within his range of capacity. If he is not, it is only through correctly diagnosing the underlying cause that appropriate intervention can be employed and success attained.

Recognizing Signs of Underachievement

The first step in determining whether your child is an underachiever is recognizing the early signs of underachievement. This task is not always easy. The younger your child, the more difficult it is to determine whether his behavior is a sign of underachievement or simply a matter of immaturity.

Often you, the parent, are the first person to suspect a problem in your child. You see him at play, during daily routines, at work, and in sleep. No one else has this opportunity. Because you see him in all aspects of his life, you know him better than anyone else. There is no teacher, pediatrician, or mental health worker who knows more about your child than you do. You can provide professionals with an enormous amount of valuable information. The more clearly you present this information to the professional working with your son or daughter, the better that person will understand your concerns. Use the check lists provided at the end of each chapter, and keep a notebook of behaviors which bother you, noting when and where they occur. Children do not act the same in all situations. Clarifying where, when, and how your youngster behaves in ways that concern you increases the probability of an accurate diagnosis. You save time and money when you accurately and definitely describe the problem that you see.

Sometimes we parents are concerned about behaviors which may, in fact, be normal aspects of a child's development. When we take accurate information to the pediatrician, teacher, or mental health worker, they can assure us that the behavior is transitional, alert us to potential problems and how to alleviate them, or provide intervention so that the problem is handled as early and efficiently as possible.

Young children are filled with energy and enthusiasm. They run, climb, jump, and tumble. Preschoolers are curious. They watch carefully what is happening around them, and they ask questions. They are learning how their world and those in it operate. They are interested in coloring, cutting, sorting, putting together puzzles, building blocks, and stringing beads. Many like playing with tiny objects. If your young child lacks enthusiasm and motivation, is inattentive, seems clumsy in large-muscle activities like running and climbing, or lacks fine motor coordination in activities like coloring or cutting, he may be at risk for a learning problem which could result in underachievement.

Of course, all children go through a learning period with new activities, and some awkwardness is to be expected. Likewise, children are not always enthusiastic nor do they always pay attention to what is happening in their environment. The at-risk child is the one who exhibits these symptoms regularly.

If your toddler or preschooler does not seem to be developing as you think he should, gather accurate information and seek advice. You will end up feeling reassured there is not a problem or reassured that you caught a potential problem early. Either way, you and your young child end up winners.

If you have a school-age child, there are more obvious clues that indicate he is having, or is at risk for, lack of academic success. The first is the report card. Although not always a reliable indicator of a child's ability, a drop in grades is a sign that something is amiss. If you find yourself constantly nagging your youngster to do his homework, perhaps motivation is an issue. "Joe never does his homework without us telling him he has to," complained Mrs. Adams. "He just fiddles around. We almost always end up yelling and screaming at each other." Children are frequently less interested in doing their homework than parents are in having them do it. The successful student knows homework is part of his life. He may procrastinate and complain about it but usually ends up getting it done. The underachiever is rarely self-motivated when it comes to homework.

When night after night your youngster tells you he does not have homework, you need to be alerted to a possible problem. Even primary grade students have homework several days a week. After third grade, homework is a daily reality. The child who never has homework is either not listening in class to know his assignments or is purposely avoiding his responsibility. Either of these situations is a clue for you.

When your seven-year-old cries before leaving for school each day, when your teenager regularly misses the bus, or when your youngster often "doesn't feel good" on week days, he is giving you a clue that something about school is not working for him. Even children who are not enthusiastic about getting up and out to school each morning know it's an unavoidable part of life. They muster the energy to make it without too much grumbling. The child and adolescent who create roadblocks to getting there are the ones to be concerned about.

Since you are probably not only a parent but also hold a job outside the home, you do not always know whether your offspring is doing what he says he is. When you ask, "Did you finish your homework?" more than likely you get a "Yup," or an "I didn't have any." When inquiring about his day or interesting activities in school, a response of, "It was okay" or "Just the regular" may be all you get. Quite possibly, you first become aware your child is not doing well in school when the teacher sends you a note, calls to tell you she is concerned, or tells you at a parent conference.

Teachers do not always know why a student is not successful. They just know he isn't. Even if the teacher has a good idea why your son or daughter is not succeeding in school, she will probably not give a diagnosis but will talk about the problem in general terms. She will make statements like, "Jason seems immature," or "I'm sure Sonia could do better if she put her mind to her work." Other phrases used to describe children with achievement problems are "not working up to potential," "underachieving," and "not doing as well as could be expected." What each of these messages means is that the teacher has some reason to believe that your son or daughter could do better in school.

The information you receive from the teacher can be confusing. It probably creates more questions than it answers. Will he outgrow his immaturity? Why can't she concentrate? How do I know he's not working up to potential? The teacher often has these same questions.

The remainder of this book will answer these questions for you. Chapters 3 and 4 lead you, step by step, through the diagnostic process necessary in determining why your child is underachieving. This information is important for any parent. Regardless of why your child is not succeeding, the process of diagnosing the problem is essentially the same for all cases. Correct diagnosis is the key to correct remediation. Know how to get that for your child. Chapters 6 through 10 discuss in detail each of the underlying causes of underachievement and what can be done about them. Chapter 11 reviews the steps necessary in getting help for your underachiever.

Who Is the Underachiever?

There are two categories of underachievement, transitory and chronic. The histories of children exhibiting each type differ as does the progression of the symptoms.

> Sara was a bright 12-year-old. She was an
> A and B student. She was well liked by her peers
> and a class leader. For six weeks she had failed
> to turn in her homework regularly. Her weekly test
> scores were erratic. In a conference with the school
> counselor, she revealed that her parents were
> getting divorced. "They both want me to live
> with them. How can I choose?" she sobbed.

Sara was a transitory underachiever. Her inability to turn in homework and perform consistently on tests was a result of conflict within her family. When she adjusted to the divorce and her new living situation, her achievement returned to the pre-trauma level.

Transitory underachievement is of relatively short duration, with a specific event preceding the onset. Children experiencing transitory underachievement need guidance and support. Illness in the child or a family member, death of a relative, home conflicts, or a move are events in the child's life which can lead to transitory underachievement. Sometimes short-term counseling is necessary to help the child cope with the stresses he is experiencing. Often children adjust to the stresses life brings without outside intervention. Loving support and time are the healers.

> Seventeen-year-old John, a high school senior, entered the office and slouched into a chair. His parents sat stiffly on the couch at the opposite side of the room. Glaring at his son, Mr. Thomas began listing John's offenses. He was getting several Ds and Fs and had been since fifth grade. He was cutting classes regularly. He did not do any chores around the house. He was disrespectful toward his family.
> "That's not true. You don't understand. You're always on me about stuff," yelled John.
> Mrs. Thomas began to cry. "We just know he won't graduate. We don't know what to do."

John was a chronic underachiever. Although his parents remembered that he had started having trouble in fifth grade, there had, in fact, been evidence since kindergarten that he was a troubled child who was not performing as well as his bright-normal ability. Because intervention had not been employed, John was barely getting by in school. Each year was less successful than the one preceding.

Chronic underachievement is a progressive process. Signs are often present early in life. Future underachievement is fostered each year in which the child experiences lack of or marginal success. It is only through correctly diagnosing the underlying cause and employing the appropriate intervention that the cycle can be broken and progress made.

Who Isn't an Underachiever?

Is this a ridiculous question? No! We all believe our children are achieving and successful if they are making A and B grades, are happy with themselves and their social relationships, and are generally content with their lives. What about the child who is content, works hard, has a successful social life, and is making Cs?

> Tori was an only child and the apple of her
> parents' eye. She was in the third grade and
> liked school. In music and P.E. Tori got As.
> In spelling she got Bs. In reading, social studies,
> science, and math, she got Cs. Her parents were
> concerned because "she seemed like such a
> bright child." She had reached developmental
> milestones early. She walked at ten months, talked
> in sentences at twenty months, and did pre-academic
> tasks at four. She was a social child who was
> well liked by both peers and adults.
>   An individually administered intelligence
> test indicated that Tori fell within the average
> area of intellectual functioning. An achievement
> test showed that all her academic skills were at
> grade level.

Tori was a strong grade-level student. She was not an underachiever nor did she have disabilities in any of the academic areas. It could be expected that she would progress successfully through school.

All children are not A and B students. The majority of people fall into what is called the average area of intelligence. Some are above average, a few are superior. Some are below average, a few are retarded. This does not mean that the intellectually average person does not have particular strengths and talents. Neither does it mean that the person cannot excel at specific tasks. It does mean that in school, a child of "average intelligence" will probably achieve grade-level work in most academic subjects.

It is important to recognize that Cs are acceptable grades. If your child is a C student, and that is his best, he needs reinforcement and encouragement.

In some schools grades have been inflated to the point that a C is considered a "bad" grade. Children are ashamed of report cards that show Cs, and parents are disappointed and angry.

A C grade should mean that a child is doing the work expected for that particular time in that particular class. It should reveal the youngster can both understand and apply the academic material. His effort may be outstanding and needs to be recognized in a separate grade; however, effort is not the same as academic ability. If you have questions about the grading policy in your child's school, ask about it.

Personality Traits of Chronic Underachievers

Each child is a unique individual with his own distinct personality. He has strengths which lead toward satisfying relationships and experiences. He also has weaknesses which, when not handled lovingly and positively, lead toward unhappiness and lack of success.

Chronic underachievers exhibit certain personality traits which contribute to their lack of success in school. Every underachiever does not possess all the characteristics; however, as a group, these children tend to show certain personality patterns. These attributes are seen in successful students as well as underachievers. The difference lies in the intensity of the expression of the trait and the extent to which it influences the child's functioning. In most children, the characteristics are temporary. In the chronic underachiever, they are integrated into the personality.

Anger and rebelliousness underlie many of the underachiever's behaviors. Sometimes the anger is expressed openly. The child is physically aggressive with both people and things. It is not uncommon to see a child rip his paper or kick his lunch pail in anger. On the other hand, the underachiever often exhibits what is called passive-aggressive behavior. This is expressing anger in indirect ways. Not studying for tests, "forgetting" homework, doing chores with minimal care or downright carelessness, and tardiness are indirect ways of showing anger.

> Lisa was 14, a beautiful girl who kept herself impeccably groomed. Her parents were professional people and both worked outside the home. According to them, they had a satisfactory relationship with Lisa and "just the normal problems."

During a consultation with Lisa and her family, her mother said, "It doesn't matter whether we're going on an errand or an outing for fun, Lisa is never ready on time. We always have to wait for her."

Lisa bristled at the comment. When asked how she felt about her mother's statement, she replied, "I have to wait for them a lot more than they wait for me. They always have to work late. They're never home when they say they're going to be."

Further exploring revealed that Lisa resented coming home to an empty house each day after school. She "felt guilty" for being mad at her parents and had never talked to them about her feelings. Her failure to get ready on time for family outings was a passive way of expressing her anger. Lisa was not consciously choosing to be late. Her unexpressed anger was dictating her behavior.

Low frustration tolerance is common to underachievers. They do not see challenges as opportunities to stretch their abilities and excel. Instead they are seen as pitfalls that lead to failure and disapproval. The child rarely sticks to a frustrating task for long.

The third grade math class was reviewing the concept of borrowing. The teacher explained each step as she worked problems on the chalk board. "Now I want you to do the rest of the problems on your own," she said.

Danny copied a problem and worked it. The second problem required borrowing from a zero. He did the problem, erased his answer, and reworked it. Again he erased his answer. He erased so hard he wore a hole through the paper. His face clouded. He wadded up the paper and shoved it into his desk with one hand while pushing his book onto the floor with the other.

Danny could not tolerate the frustration he was experiencing and was not able to seek a positive solution to his dilemma.

Underachievers are not motivated to study. They often fail to prepare for tests or complete homework. They do not like working on long-term projects and tend to do just enough to get by. They appear to live with the underlying assumption "I could do better if I tried. I just don't want to." They are rarely willing to test out their abilities. They would rather do poorly or fail by not performing than to put effort into studying and risk either success or failure.

If the underachiever studies and fails, he is confronted with the fact that he was not able to do better by trying. If he studies and succeeds, he faces a double risk. The first is that parents and teachers will establish a different set of expectations for him which he fears he cannot live up to. The second is his place in his peer group. Underachievers often choose as their friends other underachievers. If one begins to approach success as a student, he is likely to be ostracized by his group.

Underachieving children are sulky. They exhibit a sullen, morose attitude even when engaging in activities which ordinarily bring joy. Underachieving adolescents are particularly vulnerable to sulky behavior.

> Nicholas sat stiffly on the couch glaring at his mother. His lips were held tightly closed. He clenched and unclenched his fists as his mother talked.
>
> "He just never does what we ask him to do," she said. "I have to nag him about his homework constantly. He never comes home on time. And his attitude. His attitude stinks! No matter what we say, he glares at us."

The attitude Nicholas's mother referred to is one of silent resentment and protest, sulkiness. It is an aloofness. It is a barrier Nicholas put up between himself and others, primarily the adults in his life.

Stubbornness is a trait of underachievers. They push and argue with their parents, teachers, and peers. They stick to a point which opposes another even when it is to their own detriment. They argue when there is no evidence to support their position. The resulting power struggles between the adults and child frequently lead to bitter personal attacks.

The bell rang. Alex put his chair up on his desk and rushed out the classroom door. He ran to the car. "Hi, Mom! Remember we get to go and have frozen yogurt?"

"Did you bring your books out, Alex? Our plan was to go for yogurt if you remembered to bring your books home without being reminded."

"I didn't have homework today. I finished everything," said Alex.

"I know your book report isn't finished yet," Alex's mother insisted.

"It is. It is. I promise. Go ask my teacher."

Alex and his mother returned to the classroom. "Alex, you left all your books by your desk," said his teacher. "I wondered if you'd remember to come back for them. Be sure to finish your book report tonight. It's due tomorrow."

Of course, Alex did not get his frozen yogurt. More importantly, he set himself up for failure in his relationship with his mom. He did not see how his behavior contributed to the lack of trust his mother already had in him.

Underachievers are followers. They agree with whomever they are with because they do not have ideas of their own or are afraid to voice their opinions. They seek guidance from peers. They can be easily influenced and are at risk for substance abuse. Their desire to fit into a group leads them to take risks without thinking through the consequences. Under-achievers who fit this pattern are often used by their peers.

Karen regularly complained of boredom. She had difficulty finding activities she liked to do and when she did, the activity held her interest for only a short time. Even when she had friends over to her home, she was not enticed by the many games she had nor did she want to "hang out" with her friends listening to music and talking. A typical interaction went like this.

> Karen: "What do you want to do, Shelly?"
> Shelly: "I don't know. What do you have to do?"
> Karen: "Not much. What do you think?"
> Shelly: "I don't know. It's your house."
> Karen: "Hey, Mom. Can you think of anything for
> us to do? We're bored."

You might guess that anything Karen's mother suggested, if she chose to become involved in that decision, usually resulted in an, "Oh, I don't know. What do you think, Shelly?"

Underachievers have a low sense of responsibility toward themselves and others. They do not follow through on school assignments or on tasks at home. They tend to be careless with their own belongings and with those of others. Losing clothes, lunch pails, and school supplies is a common occurrence. When confronted with the irresponsibility, they become defensive. They blame peers, siblings, teachers, or parents.

> "Chad, I thought I asked you to take out the trash cans
> before dark," said Mr. Brown.
> "I couldn't, Dad. I had to go to the library."
> "Well, it wasn't dark when I got home, and you
> were already here," Mr. Brown retorted.
> "But I had to call Sandi for our English assignment,
> and she wasn't going to be home tonight. Anyway,
> you didn't remind me when you came home. You
> could have at least done that."

Chad and his father were in a discussion that led nowhere. Chad was not going to admit he had not been responsible about his chores, and his father was falling into the trap of arguing about it.

The child who is underachieving uses time poorly. He daydreams, dawdles, and procrastinates. He does not plan ahead. He does not seem to be aware of how long various activities, including routine daily tasks, take. He is easily distracted from the primary business at hand. He may or may not be aware of his inattentive behavior.

"Go and straighten your room up *now*," said Suzanne's
mother for the third time. "You have five minutes to
make your bed and put your dirty clothes in the hamper."
Suzanne stomped to her room sighing loudly. She began
picking up her clothes. Lying underneath a shirt was
the bottle of nail polish she'd been unable to find earlier.
She opened the bottle and began painting her nails.
"I thought I told you to clean your room,"
shrieked Mrs. Johnson.
"I was," yelled Suzanne. "I was picking up my clothes."

Without awareness, Suzanne had moved from picking up her clothes
to painting her nails. Mrs. Johnson believed Suzanne's behavior was
purposeful. Suzanne's inability to use time appropriately caused many
conflicts between her and her mother.

As you can imagine, the underachiever has low self-confidence and
poor self-esteem. Because he is not a successful student, he rarely gets
positive feedback in school. When asked about this, he may respond that
he does not care. You can be sure, however, that he does care and that his
confidence is undermined. Parents and teachers often see an unsuccessful
student as an unsuccessful person. The child incorporates this message and
does not value himself.

The child's self-esteem is further eroded because his relationships
within the family are impaired. He is not respected by parents or siblings.
As the case studies in this chapter indicated, nagging and arguing are the
primary means of communicating. The child feels misunderstood and is
unable to see his role in his problems.

For most youth, membership in a peer group leads to increased self-
esteem. For the underachiever, this does not happen. We choose friends
who share common interests and values with us. The underachiever is no
different. He aligns himself with other unsuccessful students. His
behaviors are accepted and encouraged by the group. Successful students
are scorned. His peer group is a fringe group that does not become involved
in the activities of the school. Such association reinforces a low concept
of self.

What Can I Do?

You now know what underachievement is, who underachieves, and what behaviors are characteristic of underachievers. If you believe your child is underachieving or is at risk, now is the time to act. Taking responsibility for finding an answer to his problem is a positive way of showing him you love him and care about his success.

The old adage "A stitch in time saves nine" is certainly appropriate to the symptom of underachievement. The sooner you recognize the problem and take the necessary steps to assist your child, the sooner he can begin to grow into a successful student. The earlier you catch the problem, the less likely it is to become severe.

The underachieving child is not a happy child. He is filled with self-doubt and conflict. Often he is confused. He is caught in a downward spiral and does not know how to help himself. Your recognition of his problem is mandatory if greater academic, social, and personal success is to be expected.

Use the check list below to rate your child's achievement level. If your child fits the pattern, do not hesitate. Use your courage and get him the help he needs. The gift each of you receives as he grows toward success is priceless.

Check List for Underachievement

Rate your child on the following traits. Remember that all children show these characteristics occasionally. This check list is to help you determine patterns you see in your child regularly. Most items on the list do not apply to preschoolers. In evaluating your very young child, refer to the section "Recognizing Signs of Underachievement" in this chapter.

	Usually	Sometimes	Rarely
1. My child appears to like school.			
2. My child attends school regularly.			
3. My child brings home his homework.			
4. My child does his homework without parental nagging.			
5. My child is able to complete his homework with minimal parental help.			
6. My child talks to me about school.			
7. Teachers, including preschool and kindergarten, have indicated concern about my child's abilities, work habits, or social skills.			
8. My child receives Ds and Fs on his report card.			
9. My child is unduly stubborn.			
10. My child daydreams and dawdles.			
11. My child procrastinates.			
12. My child does not follow through on class assignments or chores at home. continued . . .			

	Usually	Sometimes	Rarely
13. My child has difficulty understanding directions.			
14. My child does not plan ahead.			
15. My child is highly critical of others.			
16. My child blames others for his problems.			
17. My child has excuses for whatever does not work in his life.			
18. My child's friends are not successful academically or socially.			
19. My child is hostile.			
20. My child does not trust others.			
21. My child is selfish at the expense of others.			
22. My child does not accept affection.			

If most of the checks are in the *Usually* column on numbers 1-6 and in the *Rarely* column on numbers 7-22, your child is not an underachiever.

If most of the checks are in the *Sometimes* column on the entire list, your child is at risk and should be monitored closely. Use the check list on a regular basis, follow his school progress, and alert the pediatrician about any concerns as they arise.

If most of the checks are in the *Rarely* column on numbers 1-6 and in the *Usually* column on numbers 7-22, your child is showing signs of underachievement and should be evaluated both medically and education-ally-psychologically. Make appointments with the pediatrician and school counselor to discuss your concerns. Read chapters 3 and 4 before the appointments. Write down the points you want to cover in each confer-ence. Have a list of specific questions you want answered.

3

The Medical Evaluation

When your youngster was a baby, do you remember taking him to the pediatrician or family physician for his well-checks? There was a sense of anticipation. During these visits, you learned how much weight he had gained and how much longer he had grown. The many questions you had about his eating, sleeping patterns, and growth and development were answered. Here was someone who was interested in you and your growing baby. He treated your concerns with respect, and you trusted him. When the doctor told you that the baby was doing fine, you were reassured. If the baby was not doing well, you knew the physician was on your team working with your baby and you.

Whether your baby was easy or difficult, your fears and concerns were shared with an understanding person. Through the knowledge you gained and by handling your feelings as they arose, you were freed to love and take joy in your baby just as he was.

As your baby grew into toddlerhood and childhood, when he was not growing physically or emotionally the way you thought he should, you continued to seek the advice and counsel of the pediatrician. More than likely, when you think your child is underachieving, the physician is the first professional you will go to.

What if you do not have a regular physician? Don't worry. This is not uncommon. Often when children have grown through toddlerhood and early childhood without serious problems parents stop taking them to the pediatrician regularly. In many health insurance plans, services are provided through HMO's and patients do not see the same doctor or health practitioner each time they go. The rise of neighborhood medical centers which provide drop-in service and extended hours on weekends have enticed many busy families away from a regular family doctor.

Whether you have a family doctor who knows your child's history, or you and your youngster are seeing a pediatrician for the first time, a medical evaluation is a wise first step in beginning to determine what is causing the underachievement.   Medical causes are usually easier to detect than emotional or thought processing disorders. The physician can confirm or rule out a medical basis for the learning problem.   Also, information gleaned from the medical evaluation is useful to mental health and learning specialists should the services of these professionals be needed.

When you seek medical assistance for underachievement, the evaluation performed by the doctor is divided into three parts: your youngster's medical history, a physical examination, and laboratory and diagnostic tests.   The medical history and physical examination will always be included in the evaluation. The doctor will order laboratory and diagnostic tests only if information from the history or physical examination warrants these procedures.

You may be surprised to learn that of the three parts of the medical evaluation, the medical history is the most important. It is through your valuable input that this step is adequately completed. When comprehensively and carefully taken, the history provides the leads to the cause of underachievement.

When you see the completed history, you will notice signs that, in retrospect, indicated the possibility of a future problem. Since you were not trained to recognize these signs, you did not know they were warnings; or if you did, perhaps no one else you spoke to about them showed concern. There is no need to feel guilty over anything the medical history reveals. Its purpose is to shed light on the current problem and point the way to a solution.

The physical examination is necessary and important in the medical evaluation. Unexpected clues to the reason your youngster is underachieving are not usually discovered, however. Let's say, for example, that the eye examination with the Snellen Eye Chart administered during the physical indicates that your child is nearsighted. Perhaps during the taking of the medical history you said that several members in your family wear glasses or that you have noticed when your son watches TV he squints or rubs his eyes excessively. In either case, the nearsightedness would not come as a total surprise to you.

Laboratory tests rarely reveal surprise diagnoses about why a child is underachieving. These diagnostic tests can provide valuable confirmation to the diagnostic impressions formed during the history-taking and physical examination. Let's continue with the example of nearsightedness. If during the physical examination your child is found to be nearsighted, he will be referred for a comprehensive eye examination by an ophthalmologist. The more comprehensive examination will yield information necessary in prescribing glasses, but, based on the information you provided in the medical history, it is highly unlikely that eye disease or a tumor will be discovered as the cause of the nearsightedness.

In the remainder of the chapter, we will describe in detail the medical history, the physical examination, and laboratory tests.

The History

Since a comprehensive and carefully taken medical history is the most likely place for clues about your child's underachievement to emerge, you are the team member who is most vital during this stage. Your role is to provide as clear and accurate information as you can to the medical professional working with you and your youngster. A careful history takes time and demands cooperation from parents, teachers, and others who may have critical knowledge about the child. Whenever possible, both parents must participate in this review.

If you adopted your baby or are raising a foster child, the information you have may be limited. If you are the natural parents you may not be able to remember or find all the information asked for. Do not be concerned. The doctor knows you may not have answers to all his questions. Do the best you can. The purpose of background information is to have as clear a picture of your child as possible. You will not be jeopardizing the diagnosis by not knowing everything.

The history covers the time from pregnancy through your child's current age. Trying to rely on your memory for all the facts you will need can feel overwhelming and result in a less than accurate history. There are ways you can get the appropriate information and verify your facts. Records can be obtained from the obstetrician you used during your pregnancy. They contain pertinent material both about your pregnancy and your youngster's birth. If you kept a baby book, facts about early development were recorded. Schools keep cumulative files on each child which have helpful information. Teachers who work with your youngster can provide current school data. Your own parents and siblings are good resources for genetic information.

Using the questionnaires we have provided at the end of each chapter will help you organize your material. Take the appropriate completed check lists with you when you see the physician. Take written documentation of behaviors you are concerned about. Take school work that shows the kinds of errors your youngster is making. Remember, you are the expert about your child's history.

During the history taking, the physician will ask you many direct questions. He will expect you to back up your responses with facts. It is easy to give general information and observations about your child's behavior, but unless the doctor knows specifics, he cannot make an accurate diagnosis or make appropriate recommendations.

Mr. and Mrs. Ruiz were having their son Manuel, a first grader, evaluated because his classroom behavior was destructive and hyperactive. To the best of their knowledge, he had not exhibited these behaviors as a kindergartner. They were concerned that something physiological had happened to change Manuel's behavior.

The physician included in the history input from both parents as well as the kindergarten and first grade teachers. Information from the kindergarten teacher revealed that Manuel had been disruptive in her class, but at the time she judged his behavior within the normal limits of "being a boy."

In the more structured first grade, with specific academic goals, Manuel's behavior interfered with his ability to learn.

The carefully taken history and the physical examination led to a diagnosis of hyperactivity. Manuel's problem was remediated and he began to achieve academically.

With Manuel's parents and teachers both participating in the history-taking, information was available that neither the parents nor individual teachers had by themselves. Specific information supplied by the kindergarten teacher clarified behavior that had, in fact, existed prior to first grade and was not due to a new problem. Through working as a team, the parents and teachers supplied the physician with the material he needed to make an accurate diagnosis.

A detailed history includes information about your pregnancy, the delivery of your baby, and the newborn's responses immediately following his birth. You will be asked questions about illnesses or trauma, either physical or mental, that you experienced during the gestation period. The doctor will want to know about prescribed and over-the-counter medications or mood-altering drugs you took while carrying the baby. He will want to know whether you had any bleeding or spotting at any time during pregnancy.

Questions about the birth itself elicit information about trauma your baby may have experienced. How long was your labor? Were you given medication? Was the birth a vaginal delivery or Caesarean section? Were forceps used? Were there any signs of fetal distress during the delivery process?

The physician will want to know the Apgar score of your newborn at one and five minutes after delivery. The Apgar Scale is used with all newborns and measures the degree to which an infant has adjusted to the birth process and life outside the uterus. The scale measures the infant's color, heart rate, reflex irritability, muscle tone, and breathing. A rating of 0, 1, or 2 is given on each of these measures for a maximum total score of 10.

You will be asked how long your infant remained in the newborn nursery, if the baby was in the intensive care unit, and whether the baby had any respiratory distress or immediate post-delivery infection. The doctor will want to know whether you nursed your newborn or he was bottle fed.

The history continues by exploring the medical and emotional background of your child during his infancy, preschool, and school-age years. In assessing the period of infancy, you will be asked about whether your baby was calm or irritable, whether he experienced severe illnesses, seizures, or hospitalizations, and about any injuries he received. You will be asked for information about feeding problems or sleep disorders. The doctor will want to know about your baby's general behavior.

Your child's social behavior is covered in the history. How did he interact with other children during his toddler and preschool years? Did he play with his peers or did he prefer playing by himself or being with his teachers or other adults? How did he respond to his teachers? How did he interact with you and his siblings? Has his behavior changed as he has grown into childhood? In what ways is it similar and how is it different?

You will be asked to provide information on your youngster's activity level both now and when he was younger. The physician will want to know about whether your toddler and preschooler was able to pay attention during activities like story time and quiet, task-oriented play. Was he able to engage himself in activities by himself or did he always need to have an adult structure activities for him? Was he able to make the transition between active and quiet times easily or did he have difficulty settling down? Now that your child is in school, is he able to attend to his classwork and homework? Does he spend time in aimless, purposeless activity or during unstructured time is he able to engage himself in activities he enjoys?

The school-age history includes information which you supply as well as data from questionnaires which the teachers are asked to fill out. The teacher's behavioral evaluation provides pertinent information about academic, social, and athletic functioning in the school setting which you do not have the opportunity to observe regularly. Information from the report card is considered in the history; however, a behavioral rating scale which covers specific academic and behavioral functioning is often more reliable and comprehensive in covering the child's work and play habits.

> Eight-year-old Jessica was brought to the physician's attention by her parents. She was a pleasant, delightful child who was cooperative, happy, and aimed to please.
>
> During kindergarten and first grade, Jessica received satisfactory grades. In second grade her report card did not reflect grade-level work. The parents were concerned

that something had happened either medically
or psychologically to their daughter between
first and second grade.

A medical evaluation, including a
detailed history, indicated Jessica had an
attention deficit disorder without hyperactivity.
She was not able to stay on task. Because
she was not a behavior problem, her
kindergarten and first grade teachers
graded strongly on effort and personality.
Her second grade teacher focused on academic
ability.

When the family was counseled and Jessica
was administered appropriate medication, her
academic skills reached grade level.

Because Jessica's medical history included questionnaires and behavior rating scales which were filled out by her teachers, the discrepancy between her grades and actual academic functioning was clarified. Time was saved, an accurate diagnosis was reached, and Jessica became an achieving and successful student.

The final phase of the history focuses on your child's genetic background. Information will be sought about family diseases and conditions such as hearing and vision problems, mental retardation, birth defects, behavior disorders, learning difficulties, neurologic diseases and conditions marked by developmental delay, and addictions. Some families do not like to discuss genetic and addiction problems that exist in their family history. To keep information hidden which could assist in releasing your child's power for success is far from being in his best interest.

When you work with the physician on the medical history, do your best to be absolutely honest and accurate. You are not going to be judged about what you did or did not do during your pregnancy or about what you have or have not done in your parenting. The goal is to help your child to release his power for success now.

The Physical Examination

It is during the physical examination that your child first becomes part of the medical evaluation process. While performing the examination, the doctor carries on a conversation with your youngster and asks him questions about his academic abilities, social activities, and behavior. This serves two purposes. It establishes rapport with the patient which helps relieve the anxiety many children feel about going to the doctor. It also provides information about your youngster's speech and language development and general reasoning capacity. During this interaction, unless the physician asks you a specific question, it is wise for you to restrain yourself from commenting on or correcting what your youngster says. This is his time for sharing who he is and how he perceives his problem. These perceptions are added to the medical history.

In examining the child, the physician looks for signs of conditions or disease that are associated with underachievement. He also looks for disabilities that in and of themselves interfere with the learning process. Sight and hearing screening tests are administered and can be a first step in ruling out or confirming physical causes of underachievement. Most physicians use the familiar Snellen Eye Chart and single tone audiometer for this part of the physical examination. When more sophisticated tests of visual and auditory functioning are necessary, an examination by an opthalmologist or audiologist is recommended. Most parents are unaware of mild or slight vision or hearing loss in their children, yet even minimal loss can result in an inability to perform well academically.

The general physical examination includes an evaluation of the heart, lungs, abdomen, ears, nose, throat, thyroid gland (size and shape), and the musculo-skeletal and nervous systems. A conscientiously administered physical examination confirms or denies potential diagnoses considered from the medical history. Although it is not usually the case, it can uncover unsuspected causes for the underachievement.

Following the physical examination, the doctor reports his findings to you and makes his recommendations. When necessary, he refers the child for diagnostic and laboratory tests.

Diagnostic and Laboratory Tests

Routine lab work, such as a urinalysis and blood count, is frequently done in the doctor's office as part of the physical examination. Occasionally information from the medical history and physical examination demands special laboratory or diagnostic tests which require the services of specialists. These are generally performed as out-patient services in a hospital or speciality lab. If the history and physical examination were meticulously performed, these specialized electro-diagnostic, x-ray, or blood tests rarely reveal surprise leads to a diagnosis indicating under-achievement. Laboratory tests are used to support or confirm findings from the history and physical examination. A detailed laboratory search for abnormalities not based on information generated by the history and physical is not in the child's best interest nor is it a wise investment of time or money.

> Suzanne woke up many mornings with a stomach-ache. She cried because her stomach hurt and she did not want to go to school.
> Following a physical examination, her concerned parents were disturbed when the pediatrician did not recommend x-ray studies of Suzanne's abdomen. From the information gleaned from the history and physical examination, he felt certain her stomachaches were due to emotional causes. He referred Suzanne to a mental health professional for evaluation.

Many children complain of stomachaches and headaches for which no physical findings are noted. Unless these symptoms are incapacitating or supported by positive findings on the physical examination, such procedures as CT scans, upper GI studies, barium enema x-rays, or multiple blood tests for liver, kidney, and endocrine functioning are not warranted. Of course, specific situations do justify specialized diagnostic and laboratory tests, and they will be ordered for your child when necessary.

After the medical history, physical examination, and necessary diagnostic and laboratory work have been completed, the physician makes his recommendations based on his findings. If you have questions that you have not asked during the medical evaluation process, now is the time to ask. The doctor cannot know your concerns or areas in which you are confused or uncertain unless you tell him. No question is too unimportant for him to clarify for you.

When children are underachieving, the physician usually recommends the services of other team members such as the mental health specialist or educational therapist. With your permission, he shares his findings with this team member, and the next step in the discovery of what is causing your child's underachievement, or in remediating, it begins. Your willingness to take this next step with your child is your loving commitment to assist him in releasing his power for success.

Check List for the Medical Evaluation

The following check list will assist you in determining whether the medical evaluation your child received was comprehensive enough to help determine the cause of his underachievement. If you discover areas that were not addressed in the evaluation, discuss your concerns with the examining physician. You may want to take the list with you.

	Yes	No
1. The evaluating physician spent time taking a detailed history involving: a. Pregnancy		
b. Labor and delivery		
c. Newborn course		
d. Infancy		
e. Toddlerhood		
f. School-age years		
g. Familial or inherited conditions		
h. Family history of birth defects and mental retardation		
2. The physician probed into my statements to differentiate assumptions and opinions from facts.		
3. The physician got historical information from teachers and other care givers through question-naires or direct contact.		
4. The physician did a complete physical examination including the nervous system.		
5. Laboratory tests were done based on leads from the history or physical.		
6. The results of the physical examination were explained to me in terms I understood.		
7. The results of the physical examination were explained to my child in terms he understood.		

continued . . .

	Yes	No
8. All my questions were answered to my satis-faction.		
9. Recommendations for assessment by a mental health professional or educational therapist were made, based on findings from the medical evaluation.		
10. Reasons for the referral to these professionals were clearly stated.		
11. A diagnosis was arrived at before any medical therapy (such as medication) was instituted.		
12. I felt the physician really understood the problem facing my child, his teacher, and me as a result of his underachievement.		
13. A concise and clear plan of action was given to me, both verbally and in writing.		

4

The Educational and Psychological Evaluation

Each of us is a multidimensional being made up of a physical body, an intricate nervous system, and emotions. In determining the cause for underachievement and developing a means for correcting the problem, the whole child must be carefully studied; his body, nervous system, thinking, and emotions—each plays a role in his inability to learn effectively. In the last chapter, we discussed the medical evaluation which focuses on the physical body. In this chapter, we talk about the educational and psychological evaluation which is primarily concerned with the thought processes and emotions.

Because you love your child and are seeking answers to assist him in releasing his inherent power for success, this is the next step you will take. The process takes longer than the medical evaluation, but, without it, the information you received from the physical workup is of little value. The educational and psychological evaluation reveals intellectual and emotional processes which interfere with learning and sheds light on how identified physical disorders create blocks to achievement. Most importantly, this evaluation points the way to reaching success. By the time the educational and psychological evaluation is complete, you have the information which serves as the road map for remediating the cause of your youngster's underachievement.

One of the first questions parents ask about this evaluation is "What shall I tell my child?" Always tell him the truth. Sometimes parents mistakenly believe children are not aware of their problems. Many parents say to us, "If I take my son to a psychologist, won't he think there is something wrong with him?" Of course, there is nothing "wrong" with the child; however, there certainly is something which is prohibiting him from being an effective student, and he knows it! Confronting the situation and taking the steps to correct it may be the first time his underachievement has been openly discussed in your family in a positive way.

Your youngster's age dictates the words you choose to tell him about his upcoming evaluation. In all cases, telling him what, why, when, and where are your best guidelines. For example, you might say to your seven-year-old, "Aaron, on Tuesday you and I are going to have an appointment with Mrs. Green. She works with boys and girls who have a hard time with their school work. She is going to do some activities with you that will help us know why reading is hard for you."

Most children take the information in stride and are relieved that help is on the way. The question children are most likely to ask is "Will she give me a test? I hate tests." If your youngster asks this question, you can ease his anxiety by answering, "I don't know all the things Mrs. Green does, but I understand she does fun and interesting activities with boys and girls." Each mental health and educational therapist handles the issue of testing in her own way. Each knows that children who are not successful students are afraid of tests. You can rest assured that your child will be made to feel at ease during the evaluation, and that most of the tests are presented in an interesting way. Nearly all therapists include fun activities as part of the evaluative procedure.

Perhaps your youngster is having his evaluation through his school. You may not know exactly when it will take place. Prepare him for the future event by letting him know that the school psychologist will be calling him to her office and why. Say something like, "Miss Blair, your school psychologist, will be calling you into her office soon. She will do some activities with you which will help us understand why reading is hard for you."

It is important that you have an understanding about what an educational and psychological evaluation entails. You will feel more comfortable about taking your child to the therapist or having him evaluated at his school if you know what goes on behind the closed doors. Yes; although you will be asked to participate in the initial interview, you will not be allowed to remain in the room during the evaluation.

In the remainder of this chapter, we are going to tell you what your child is doing during the evaluation and what you will learn from the results. We will be using three words many times—*testing*, *evaluating*, and *diagnosing*. Each of these words refers to the process of identifying your child's problem. *Testing* means the actual administering of the tests, *evaluating* refers to the process the therapist goes through when analyzing the data, and *diagnosing* is the interpreting and labeling of the results. The entire process is called an evaluation or diagnostic workup.

Your Child's Rights to Evaluation

As parents, you have two options when your child needs an educational and psychological evaluation. Testing can be done through the public schools or through private professionals.

In 1977, Congress passed the Education for All Handicapped Children Act, Public Law 94–142 (PL 94–142). The law went into full effect in September 1978. This law states that public schools must meet all the educational needs of all the pupils served by the school free of cost. This includes evaluation and appropriate educational placement of the child. If you have chosen to send your child to a private school, you still have the right to request and receive evaluation and services through the public school district in which you live.

> Jeff was a second-grade student in a parochial school. He was working below grade level in reading and language arts. He was depressed and unwilling to complete his classwork or homework. The school did not have a psychologist or learning specialist on the staff. The parents requested testing through their neighborhood public school.
>
> Jeff was tested by a district psychologist and diagnosed as having a learning disability in written language. His parents wanted to keep him in the parochial school, even though it was not equipped to provide the necessary services to remediate his disability.
>
> The school district provided bus service to a resource room at a nearby public school, where Jeff received

one hour of special help each day. He was then
returned to his parochial school. All services were
provided to Jeff free of cost under PL 94–142.

Like many parents, Jeff's parents were unaware that services for their
son were available. They took him to a private therapist who could see that
a complete evaluation and follow-up therapy would be a financial strain for
the family. She taught them how to take the steps necessary in securing
their son's rights and participated in the process. The school district was
highly cooperative, and Jeff made fine progress in his resource room.

Public schools have programs for the communicatively disabled,
physically disabled, learning and emotionally disabled, severely disabled,
and for those with multi-disabilities. If a child has a disability that cannot
be met through the public school district, the district is required to fund the
child's education elsewhere.

Although PL 94–142 has provided parents with a powerful tool for
gaining services for their learning-impaired child, it is often a frustrating
experience trying to get a child tested through the school system. Frequently, parents are required to go through unnecessary red tape to get the
services their child deserves. District budgets are tight, psychologists have
large caseloads, and it is not always easy to prove that the child really needs
an evaluation. Like all laws, PL 94–142 has loopholes which can be
conveniently used by districts. Nonetheless, with persistence, parents can
usually get the evaluation process started. Discuss your concerns and
desires with your youngster's classroom teacher. Ask her if she believes
your son or daughter has a learning problem which would benefit from
specialized educational services; if so, ask that she request an evaluation
with the appropriate school personnel. You can send a written request for
evaluation to the school principal or counselor. In your letter, state why you
are asking for services. Requesting the services of an independent
professional as an advocate sometimes hastens the process. Parent
advocates and legal advocates are available.

Once an evaluation by the school district has been approved, most state
laws require that the evaluation and proper placement for the child be
completed within a certain time frame. This is usually between 30 and 60
working days.

Private Evaluations

When you choose to have your youngster evaluated by a private professional, you rarely have to wait long for the process to begin. The evaluation itself, however, will take longer than if it is done through the school district. This is because private therapists usually do a more in-depth evaluation, and they often work with a child for no more than an hour at a time. School psychologists usually need to complete an evaluation in one sitting because of the large numbers of students they must serve.

If you have the opportunity to speak to the therapist when you call to make the initial appointment, she will discuss her fees with you and what those fees cover. If you do not speak to her, ask the secretary who takes your call about the fee schedule. Also ask whether insurance customarily covers any portion of the costs. It is helpful if you have the name of your insurance company available and know whether your policy covers mental health services. The fees you pay for an evaluation depend on who does the workup, the time involved, how complete the evaluation is, and where you live. Most therapists charge on an hourly basis; however, some have a flat fee. If the fee you are quoted seems outrageous, call two or three other professionals in the field and ask what their fees are as a comparison. Some therapists work on a sliding fee scale. Most will work out a payment schedule that is comfortable for you. Remember, the time the therapist is with your child is only a portion of the time she spends on his case. She will work anywhere from five to ten hours interpreting the testing data, making a diagnosis, and writing the evaluation report. Do not, under any circumstances, use someone's services just because their fees are lower than someone else's. By the same token, do not assume that higher fees mean better service.

The physician who performed the medical evaluation will probably recommend a learning specialist or mental health therapist to you. If he does not, schools usually have a number of professionals they use as referrals. In choosing the therapist you work with, make sure the person has knowledge of and experience with both learning and emotionally impaired children. She should be willing to observe your child in his school setting either before or during the evaluation. She should work with you and the school to ensure appropriate educational intervention following the evaluation if it is warranted.

During the first appointment you have with the therapist, you and your child are both invited into her office. Usually she wants to know what both you and your son or daughter perceive the problem to be. During this interview, she establishes rapport with you and your youngster and begins to see how the two of you interact with each other. She will probably begin the testing during this first appointment.

An adequate evaluation to determine the cause of underachievement takes from five to seven hours. This includes the initial session and a session following the testing to discuss the results and recommendations. The school observation is not included in this time frame. The number of hours the testing itself takes depends on your child's age, his abilities, his attention span, and the number of tests the examiner gives. This varies among therapists. Mental health and learning specialists have chosen batteries or groups of tests they administer. Information gleaned from one test may lead them to add to or delete from that battery. Certain areas of your child's functioning will always be tested. Others are tested only if the need is indicated. A complete evaluation, including the school observation, should not take more than a total of eight hours.

After all testing is completed, the therapist sits down with your child and tells him in words he comprehends what his problem is and how he can be helped. He should not be given number scores or labels. He needs to be told and shown with examples what has prohibited successful learning, what can be done, and his role in the process. The therapist also has a conference with you and gives you a detailed explanation of the results. You will have many questions. She will answer them in such a way that you understand the problem. If you do not, ask the question again. It may be necessary to ask the same question several times. You will receive lots of information, and it can be confusing. It is not foolish to repeat a question or seek clarification on information. It is important that you grasp what the evaluation reveals.

As interesting as the findings may be, the most important part of this conference is the recommendations the therapist makes. At least half of the conference hour should be spent in discussing her recommendations. An evaluation without a plan for correcting any discovered causes for your child's underachievement is a waste of your money. A diagnosis in itself is worthless.

After the completed evaluation, you should be given a written report including evaluation results and the recommendations discussed with you. You may not receive it the very day of your conference, so ask when you will receive it. When you read the report, you may not understand all of it, since professional jargon is often used. Do not feel bothered by this. The therapist told you everything she learned about your youngster in your conference with her. The report is primarily for use by the school and other professionals who will be working with him. Your copy is your record for your files.

The therapist will ask you to sign an information release form so that a copy of the report can be sent to those who will work with your child. Sometimes it takes several weeks from the time a request is made until the information is received. To save time, you may wish to provide a copy of your own report. Records of the evaluation will be kept by the service provider for a number of years.

The Evaluation Procedure

In the following sections we discuss the evaluation procedure and what the various tests measure and mean. The same kinds of tests are used in an evaluation by the school district or by a private professional. Some of the information will seem complicated. Nonetheless, we have presented the material to you because we believe you have the right to know as much as possible about the process of releasing your youngster's power for success, and this testing is a crucial part of that process.

The evaluation includes tests which determine how your child functions in six developmental areas: general intellectual functioning, academic achievement, language skills, perceptual skills, sensory-motor skills, and social-emotional behavior. An evaluation may be either complete or partial. A complete evaluation covers all six areas. A partial evaluation includes testing in one or several, but not all, categories. It is important that the evaluation be complete enough to correctly diagnose the disability leading to underachievement so that appropriate intervention can be initiated. Over-evaluating serves no purpose, however.

Both formal and informal means of gathering information are used. Formal or standardized tests are carefully researched on thousands of people before they are used as diagnostic tools. They are based on norms or statistics which tell how well a typical group of children of the same age did on the test. The results your child receives on a standardized test are compared to the norms developed for that test. They are expressed as an IQ (Intelligence Quotient), grade-level, percentile, or standard score. Each of these number scores indicates how your child achieved in comparison with other children his age.

Informal tests are not standardized. They give information about your child himself, but this information is not compared to findings on other children. The results are usually not given in number scores but in statements about his performance. "Matthew recognizes the colors red, green, blue, and yellow," or "Anna is able to recall and accurately repeat a four-word sentence" are statements illustrating the kinds of information informal diagnostic measures give. This type of information can be used to compare your child's ability at different points in time.

A school or in-office observation is an informal diagnostic tool. The observer takes minute-by-minute notes on your youngster's behavior over a given period of time, usually an hour. The observation notes provide information on his ability to attend to task, activity level, social skills, academic skills, and language. The observer does not interpret the behavior during the observation. She simply notes the behavior as it occurs. A behavioral note might be "Jack hit Joey," not "Jack got mad at Joey."

The fact that a procedure is informal does not detract from its value. Informal tests and school or in-office observations are an essential component in your youngster's evaluation.

General Intellectual Functioning

A child's general intellectual functioning, or learning potential at the time he is tested, is measured by a standardized test called an intelligence scale or test, IQ test, or test of mental ability. IQ stands for intelligence quotient and is the number score achieved on the intelligence scale.

The test measures a person's ability to think and reason, both verbally and nonverbally. That is, how well can he think through and give an answer orally, and how well can he do tasks which do not require verbalization.

Many parents believe an IQ score indicates how "smart" their child is. This is true in a general way; however, the IQ score itself is a composite score which is derived from a number of subtests which measure different abilities. Thus, it does not tell how "smart" a child is in reference to particular types of tasks.

Only certain thinking skills are measured on the IQ test. Creativity, personality factors, artistic talents, and athletic skills are not overtly measured. One psychologist and researcher, J.P. Guilford, identified at least 120 kinds of thinking abilities. The most commonly used IQ tests measure only 10 to 12 of these.

When a child's IQ is measured, it is important to keep in mind that there is more to him and his abilities than the single IQ score. The IQ number itself is relatively meaningless. What is important is the pattern of his abilities as measured by the different subtests, and how well he is able to use the thinking skills he has.

Any adequate evaluation will include an intelligence test. Two tests which are highly suited to determining the cause of learning problems are the Wechsler Intelligence Scale for Children—Revised, commonly called the WISC—R, and the Stanford-Binet Intelligence Scale.

The WISC—R is a particularly useful test for diagnosing learning problems. It is standardized for use with children from six through 16 years of age. It consists of 12 subtests grouped between a verbal and a performance scale. The verbal tests require the child to use language. The examiner asks him questions which require a verbal response. He must speak an answer.

Performance tests require an action response. The child is given a task to complete with puzzles, pictures, or blocks. He may talk while he works, but his score is based on what he does, not on what he says. Performance tasks are usually timed tests.

The WISC—R yields three scores: Verbal IQ, Performance IQ, and Full Scale IQ. Scores from the 12 subtests can be plotted on a graph.

Comparing differences between verbal and performance skills, and comparing abilities measured by each subtest, provides the examiner with information about learning patterns. A skilled examiner can infer personality and possible organic factors from the data.

The Stanford-Binet Intelligence Scale is often referred to as the Binet. It can be used with children from two and one-half to 18 years of age. Both verbal and nonverbal skills are measured, although the test is more heavily weighted toward verbal abilities. Many evaluators feel the Stanford-Binet is not as useful for diagnosing learning problems as the WISC—R. It does not separate verbal and nonverbal skills as clearly.

The Binet yields two scores, mental age and IQ. A mental age score indicates the age at which the child is functioning intellectually. For example, if his chronological age is 10 years six months (written 10-6), and he has a mental age of 14 years two months (written 14-2), this means that, theoretically, he thinks as well as the average child of 14-2. Mental age, or MA, does not reflect life experience or social maturity. It does not mean that the 10-year-old child is as mature as the 14-year-old. Although the IQ and MA are useful indicators of a child's current potential, knowing what kinds of thinking he is strong or weak in is required to develop an adequate learning program. The test administrator will provide that information from the analysis of the subtest results.

If an at-risk preschooler is being evaluated, the Wechsler Preschool and Primary Scale of Intelligence—Revised (WWPSI—R) is frequently used. It is formatted much like the WISC—R and yields a Verbal, Performance, and Full Scale IQ.

The Peabody Picture Vocabulary Test (PPVT) is often utilized in the evaluation. It can be used with children from two and one-half to 18 years of age. The test measures the child's receptive or hearing vocabulary; the words he understands when he hears them. The examiner says a word, and the child chooses a picture from among four which best describes the word. The instrument is useful for children who have difficulty with language, since it does not require a verbal response. It provides an IQ and a mental age score. The IQ achieved on the PPVT is frequently higher than that measured by the WISC—R or Binet. Since the test is not multi-dimensional, it is not an IQ test in the true sense of the word. It is a valuable diagnostic tool but should not be used as the sole measure of intellectual ability.

Multi-dimensional nonverbal intelligence scales are available which are extremely useful in measuring the intellectual functioning of nonspeaking or language-impaired children.

Academic Achievement

Achievement tests measure how well a child has mastered the subjects commonly taught in school. Achievement test batteries evaluate more than one academic skill. Specific achievement tests analyze single skills, such as reading or math. The tests provide grade-level scores, percentile scores, and standard scores.

The grade-level score indicates whether the child is working at, above, or below his current grade in school. The percentile and standard scores are used to compare his abilities with those of other children his age. A standard score is comparable to an IQ score and provides valuable information about the child's academic ability as compared with his intellectual functioning.

In diagnosing a learning problem, it is absolutely necessary to evaluate a child's achievement skills in word recognition, oral reading fluency, oral and silent reading comprehension, phonics, spelling, ability with written language, applied math, and math computation. Some achievement tests provide information on the child's ability in social studies, science, research skills, or humanities. Although such data is interesting and gives a more complete picture of the child academically, it is not crucial to a diagnosis.

Language Skills

The child's ability to use verbal language is called *expressive* language ability. His skill in understanding spoken language is his *receptive* ability. In an evaluation to diagnose the cause of underachievement, the examiner will use both formal and informal techniques to determine a child's skill at both using and understanding language. A comprehensive speech and language assessment is undertaken only when it is deemed necessary. When a complete language evaluation is warranted, the child is referred to a speech and language specialist.

The ability to hear and use the fine differences between sounds is necessary in learning the phonics skills associated with reading. There is a much closer association between language and reading than might be expected. A child who has serious reading problems probably has some kind of language-processing problem which needs to be addressed. In such cases, a comprehensive speech and language evaluation will be recommended.

Perceptual Skills

Perceptual functioning refers to how a person uses information that comes through the senses, primarily visual, auditory, kinesthetic, and tactile. Sometimes children who underachieve are unable to read, write, or do math because of a perceptual disability.

This is a problem in which the brain does not process sensory information properly. For example, a child may have excellent vision or hearing acuity; that is, he sees and hears well. What he sees or hears, however, is not processed or interpreted by the brain correctly, so that what he does with the information he receives is faulty.

Nine-year-old Jamie had struggled with reading since first grade. She had a difficult time seeing the differences between *b* and *d* and *p*, *q*, and *g*. She read some words backwards. Her errors included *saw* for *was* and *on* for *no*. She had repeated first grade because of her reading problems, and she was considered "immature."

By the end of second grade she had shown little improvement in reading. An evaluation by a learning specialist revealed that Jamie had a visual perceptual disorder. The reversals she made would not improve if she "tried harder." She was not reading carelessly. Maturity would not solve her problem.

When she perceived or saw the letters *no* on the page, her brain processed them as *on*. Educational therapy with the learning specialist did not "cure" Jamie's disorder. It did increase her reading ability by teaching her new skills and ways to work around the disability.

Perceptual testing will always be a part of an adequate evaluation. The examiner will use both formal and informal tests. At the conclusion of the testing, she will have a clear idea about your child's receptive and expressive perceptual abilities.

Sensory-motor Skills

Sensory-motor skills are usually divided into three categories: large-muscle or gross-motor skills, small-muscle or fine-motor skills, and sensory-motor integration. Gross-motor skills include the ability to roll, sit, crawl, walk, run, throw, jump, skip, and dance. The large muscles are used in these activities.

Small muscles are used for tasks like picking up small objects, stringing beads, putting pegs in a peg board, drawing, coloring within lines, printing, and writing.

Sensory-motor integration is the integration or harmonizing of gross and fine motor activities. Included in this category are balance, perception of body in space, speed, dexterity, directionality, laterality, and tactile discrimination. Problems in these areas seem to be associated with learning problems in some children.

Many sensory-motor skills are informally studied in the evaluation. The examiner observes the child's sensory-motor abilities while he is doing other tasks. Usually a visual-motor test is given to determine how well the student can coordinate eye-hand functions, such as copying words and patterns, or copying a peg design or a bead pattern. In-depth evaluation is undertaken only if indicated. When remediation is instituted in this area, it does not cure a child's learning problems. What sensory-motor training can do for some children is make academic tasks which require eye-hand coordination easier.

Social-emotional Behavior

In evaluating a child's social-emotional behavior, the evaluator pays attention to how the child interacts with his peers, siblings, parents, and adults outside the family. She notices how the child feels about himself, how he feels about others, and how others feel about him. Attention is given to personality and temperament characteristics. Is the child anxious? Is he depressed? Is he overly compliant or obstinate? Is he withdrawn or is he excessively active? Does he have a healthy sense of worth as an individual?

A child's inner life and social life play a major role in his success as a student. The social-emotional behavior is evaluated through observation, conversation, behavior rating scales, and formal and informal tests.

Projective tests are often used to gain information about the personality. The child completes open-ended sentences, tells stories, or talks about pictures the examiner presents. His own feelings and attitudes are expressed or "projected" into his responses. There are no right or wrong answers. The examiner interprets the results in light of her understanding of psychological concepts and symbols. The degree of testing undertaken in the social-emotional realm varies among professionals. An adequate evaluation must consider the child's social-emotional functioning.

How Do I Choose?

Some of you will ask the school district to evaluate your child. Others of you will choose a private professional. Sometimes parents have their youngster evaluated by the school, then go to a private therapist for consultation about the results or for follow-up testing. Many schools do some testing of their own regardless of how thorough a job a private professional has done. Whichever route you decide to take, make sure you are comfortable with the outcome. This does not mean being comfortable with the results of the testing. The results can be confusing and sometimes disturbing. It does mean being satisfied that your child has had an evaluation thorough enough to diagnose his problem, that you have as complete an understanding of his problem as possible, and that the recommendations provided lead the way to releasing his power for success. Until the services you have sought provide these results, continue to ask for them. The check list at the end of this chapter will assist you in determining whether your youngster has received the evaluation he needs and whether your family has received the guidance necessary to take the steps needed for correcting the problem.

If you decide to have the school district perform the evaluation, the evaluator will be the district psychologist who serves your child's school. She has made a career of working with children and knows them well. If you decide to use the services of an independent professional, choose someone you can trust and who has experience working with children. The physician who did the medical evaluation, your child's school counselor, or friends and business associates who have had a positive experience with a professional are good resources.

Many of you will want to speak to the therapist before making an appointment, so that you have a feeling for what she is like. This is your right. She does not have time to talk at length on the telephone with prospective clients, so expect to get a brief description of what will take place during the evaluation and an estimate of the fee for the service. If you have questions that will take time to explore, you may be asked to schedule a consultation. Some therapists charge only a partial hourly fee for consultation appointments.

If you do not like the person you will be working with in this very important step, you will have a difficult time listening objectively to what she has to tell you about your youngster. As hard as it is to watch our children underachieve, for some of us there is a fear in finally shedding light on the problem. It means that we can no longer hope that our child will magically overcome his difficulties. You need to feel confident that the therapist and you can work together to help your offspring. Do not mistake your own anxieties about the evaluation for feelings of dislike for a therapist. Most therapists are genuinely caring people. Many who work with children are warm and nurturing. Follow your own feelings, however. Do not go to someone just because you have heard she is good.

What Should I Expect Following the Evaluation?

Whether the evaluation is undertaken in the school or privately, by its completion you will know what is causing your youngster's underachievement and what steps must be taken to remediate the problem. Rarely will there be a single cause for his difficulties with learning. Most often there is a combination of factors contributing to underachievement.

By the conclusion of the evaluation, you will know what can be done in medical, mental health, or educational therapy to assist your child to release his power for academic, social, and emotional success. You will know what kind of follow-through you will be responsible for at home. You will have some indication about how long the therapeutic process is expected to take. Growth cannot be predicted exactly, so you will be given an expected time range. Anywhere from one to three years is realistic for most cases.

The amount of information you receive can be overwhelming. Be sure to continue to ask questions until you are comfortable with your understanding of what you have been told. Many times, questions arise as the days pass after completion of the evaluation and you have time to mull over the information. Keep a list of these questions and schedule a telephone or in-office session to ask them. Perhaps of most importance, remember an evaluation is only beneficial if a careful plan of action follows the diagnosis of the problem. Knowing the problem alone is a waste of your time and money. The action following the diagnosis is crucial, and you are responsible for making sure it takes place. The physician or therapist cannot demand that you take the action steps.

Remediation, rehabilitation, and growth are a process. What happens during the process depends on the commitment of the people involved and the abilities they have. Change requires hard work. Only through the willingness of you and your child to work with the school and the other professionals involved, can change be expected.

Growth is sometimes defined as a process of taking two steps forward, then one step back. Slow progress is frustrating, yet a reality. Results mean a willingness to accept change as it occurs. Patience is a must in the process.

Now that you have read the chapters on the medical and educational-psychological evaluations, you may be getting cold feet. What is required in adequately and accurately diagnosing the reason for your youngster's underachievement seems like a monumental task. The process we have described *is* a big task. It is also efficient and ultimately saves you time and money. The cost to underachievers, their families, and society is far greater when they are allowed to drift through school undiagnosed and untreated than when the appropriate steps are taken as soon as you believe your child is having problems.

If your youngster's teeth were causing him pain or if he had a physical disease, you would do whatever you needed to do to bring him back to health. Learning problems cause deep and life-long pain. Exercise your love through action and take the step toward evaluation and treatment for your underachiever. The process can fail only if the step is never taken.

Check List for the Educational-psychological Evaluation

The items on this check list will help you determine whether the evaluation administered to your child was sufficient and met your expectations. If it did not, ask for the services you did not receive from the educational or mental health therapist. You may want to take the list with you.

	Yes	No
1. I had an interview with the psychologist or learning specialist in which my child's history and my perceptions of the problem were discussed.		
2. Before the evaluation, the psychologist or learning specialist asked my child about his perceptions of the problem.		
3. I was apprised of the approximate cost of the evaluation prior to testing.		
4. I was informed about approximately how long the evaluation would take prior to testing.		
5. A school observation was done on my child.		
6. After the evaluation, I was told the nature of my child's disability in terms I understood.		
7. I received information about my child's: a. Intellectual functioning		
b. Academic achievement		
c. Language skills		
d. Perceptual skills		
e. Sensory-motor skills		
f. Social-emotional behavior		
8. I was given recommendations for remediating the problem. continued . . .		

	Yes	No
9. I was given a written report summarizing the evaluation.		
10. All my questions were answered straight-forwardly and in terms I understood.		
11. My child was told what was impairing his learning in terms he understood.		
12. My child was told how he could be helped and what his responsibility in the process would be.		
13. All my child's questions were answered in terms he understood.		

5

Treatment

Now the groundwork is laid. You and your youngster have completed the first three steps toward releasing his power for success. Initially, you recognized that a problem existed. Through your own observations, through input from his teacher, or both, you reached the conclusion that your child was not achieving as well in school as you thought he could or should. Next, you discussed your concerns with your family doctor. You prepared yourself for this step by organizing the information you observed through using the check list provided in chapter 1. You listed the questions you had about the behaviors you observed and about the nature of the problem. Finally, you made the arrangements, and your youngster was evaluated medically, educationally, and psychologically. The purpose of these evaluations was to determine what was causing the underachievement. Now you know. A diagnosis has been made and recommendations have been presented to you.

Whether you are aware of it or not, throughout this process you have been accomplishing two more steps necessary in releasing the power for success. You have been learning to be an effective consumer of professional services, and to assertively ask for services you are not getting and believe you should receive. In your reading of chapters 1 through 4, and in using the check lists, you have raised your consumer awareness and gained the knowledge necessary for courageous action. Believe it or not, each of the steps you have taken so far has been the action of a loving parent! Some of you are thinking that is not really true. You think the only reason you started this long and involved process is because you were desperate. You were. Most of us feel desperate at various times throughout our years of parenting. Some of us wait to take action until we are desperate. Each of us knows it is sometimes hard to love our children just the way they are. Disappointment, fear, and anger get in the way of our ability to feel and express love. Regardless of how you *think* you feel about your underachiever, your *actions* toward helping him release his power for success show caring, concern, and faith in him and his abilities. Now it is time to take the next step.

This step requires following through on the recommendations made by the physician and educational or mental health therapist. It is the treatment phase. Treatment is also called *remediation* or *intervention*. Although the terms are used interchangeably, treatment usually refers to medical and psychological assistance, while remediation is educationally based. Intervention refers to any process of intervening, breaking into, or interrupting the process which is detrimental to the individual—in this case, underachievement.

Treatment can be medical, educational, psychological, or any combination of the three. It may last several months or several years. Some aspects of medical treatment, such as prescribed medication, may be necessary for many years. Certainly the skills and insights learned during educational and psychological intervention must be regularly incorporated into daily living practices for continued effectiveness.

You know from reading chapters 1, 3, and 4 that effective treatment is based on accurately diagnosing the medical, educational, and psychological causes for underachievement. Effective treatment also requires something else. It requires commitment on the parts of you and your youngster.

As relieved as you are to know what is causing your child's lack of school success, this knowledge alone does nothing to solve his problem. Even knowing how to solve the problem is valueless unless you act on that knowledge. This action is your commitment to follow through on the recommendations made during the medical and educational-psychological evaluations.

Most parents do not have trouble making the initial commitment to treatment because most of us truly believe that we would do almost anything to assist our floundering child. When that commitment impinges on our own lives, when it requires us to look at our family structure and perhaps modify it, when it requires us to learn and implement new parenting skills, and when the treatment process does not move as quickly as we wish, our commitment is put to the test.

In order for our underachieving children to become successful, we must examine any resistances we may have to the treatment process, put aside our preconceived notions, and enter into it ourselves fully and with commitment. No therapist or physician, no matter how skilled, can release a child's power for success for him. It demands committed team effort by the parents, the child, and all professionals working with him.

In chapters 6 through 10, we explore in detail five disorders that result in underachievement: Attention deficit disorder with hyperactivity, attention deficit disorder without hyperactivity, learning disability, emotional disorders, and low IQ. The first two, attention deficit disorder with and without hyperactivity, are primarily medically based problems. Treatment almost always includes the services of the physician as well as educational and mental health professionals. Learning disability, emotional problems, and low IQ are primarily educationally and psychologically based. The primary providers of service will come from the educational and mental health professions, although the physician may also be involved in treatment. Chapters 6 through 10 provide a medical, educational, and psychological picture of the child exhibiting the disorder resulting in underachievement, and also explore parenting skills and common methods of medical, educational, and psychological intervention which are particularly effective with each child. The information we offer is not comprehensive. Books have been written by the score on each individual disorder. Our purpose is to give you the information you need to assist in identifying your youngster's problem, to understand his problem so that you can support and guide him in releasing his power for success, and to become an effective consumer of the services available to your family.

When a diagnosis is made, a label is assigned to a disorder. That is, the disorder is given a name. Labels are efficient because they allow us to discuss the common characteristics of a group of individuals. They serve as a guide for treatment. They are used as a means for appropriate educational programming. They are necessary for insurance coverage. Labels can be dangerous, however, because they group people into categories. It is easy to lose sight of an individual's particular traits and needs and see only those characteristics which fit the label. Parents, teachers, physicians, and mental health professionals must keep aware that we are *always* dealing with individuals. We are *never* working with a label. For example, while children with learning disabilities have common characteristics, each child with a learning disability is unique in his own combinations of strengths and weaknesses. It is important to remember that your youngster *has* a disability that results in underachievement. *He* is not the disability. In the following chapters we deal with labels. We present information that is common to groups of children exhibiting attention deficit disorder with and without hyperactivity, learning disability, emotional problems, and low IQ. Although their names and other identifying characteristics have been changed, the case studies are stories of individual children in our practices who have had these problems leading to underachievement. Your child may or may not exhibit the characteristics we describe. More than likely, he will show some or similar traits if he has the disorder. His treatment program will be individual to him. It will be similar to that of another child with the disability but not exactly the same.

In discussing the intervention program for children exhibiting an attention deficit disorder with or without hyperactivity, we talk about the use of medication as part of the treatment for some children. The pros and cons of using medications in controlling the symptoms of these disorders have been covered extensively through the media. Our position is not one of being either for or against medication. We believe that each case must be evaluated individually and a decision made for that particular child. We know that medication is not a cure-all. We know that some children do not respond to medication, even if our clinical judgment indicates they should. We also know that, for optimal success, some children require medication. If medication is considered for one of our patients or clients, it is only prescribed after a monitored medication trial. When prescribed, regular evaluation of the efficacy and dosage of the medication is always necessary. We believe this procedure is mandatory when medication is used as part of the treatment process.

Now, as you learn about each of the disorders that can result in underachievement, we once again suggest that you use the check lists at the ends of the chapters to assist you in observing your youngster more objectively and in evaluating the services he is or will be receiving.

6

The Child with an Attention Deficit Disorder with Hyperactivity

Healthy children are active. They are exuberant. They run, they talk in loud voices, and they appear to have endless energy. They are not often aware of becoming tired and resist the requests of guiding parents to quiet down. When they become over-activated, it takes them time to settle into a quiet time. These same energetic children enjoy sitting and listening to stories or watching TV. They pay attention in school. They respond to discipline by parents and teachers. They have friends and recognize, even though they may not be able to verbalize it, that relationships require mutual giving and respect.

We have worked with many families who have thought they had a hyperactive child. They have been unaware of the wide continuum of behavior that is considered normally active. Some of these parents have been resentful that effective parenting takes so much time and energy. They have felt that if their youngster "could be calmed down" their job would be easier. Sometimes they have compared their offspring to other children and felt cheated that their child was harder to handle. Usually these parents have been tired from the many roles they balance in their lives and concerned because they do not feel effective in their parenting of their active youngster.

Only a small percentage of children have an activity level that is higher than normal. This excessively active behavior is technically labeled attention deficit disorder with hyperactivity. It is commonly referred to simply as hyperactivity, and that is how we refer to it throughout this chapter. Hyperactive behavior is purposeless. It is primarily random motion not directed toward a specific end.

If your child is hyperactive, he runs in high gear most of the time. He is so full of undirected energy he is not easy to live with. You are exhausted trying to stay ahead of him and frustrated because he does not respond to your attempts at effective parenting. You are frightened by his impulsive behavior. You are humiliated because in public people respond to you as if you are an incompetent parent. You are angry because you feel trapped. Few people understand your dilemma.

You, like many parents, may have a hard time feeling love for your hyperactive child. It is deeply hidden beneath your pain. You probably feel totally consumed by this youngster. Not only is he difficult to parent, it is not easy to get space away from him. Grandparents and other family members may not offer to care for him the way they do for other children in the family. Even when you can find a sitter who will stay with him, you have a hard time relaxing on an evening out because you are worrying about what is happening at home. The hyperactive child is rarely invited to other children's homes to play and children are not eager to come to his house. The burden of the child's behavior rests almost solely on you.

The hyperactive child is challenging to you. Your relationship with him is far from satisfying, and, believe it or not, it is not satisfying to him either. He threatens much of your esteem surrounding your parenting. He is challenging to his teachers. They do not want him in class because he is too disruptive. They are frustrated because he is not responsive to their disciplinary attempts.

The child is a puzzle to himself. Why do I always get in trouble, he wonders. Why am I the one who always gets caught? What's wrong with me? Why don't I have friends?

The hyperactive child needs help desperately if he is to become successful at home, in school, and socially. A team approach with the child, you, the classroom teacher, the physician, mental health professional, and educational therapist is required to correctly identify the basis of the hyperactivity and plan appropriate treatment.

Characteristics of the Hyperactive Child

> Erik blew into the classroom like a hurricane,
> legs and arms flying, whistling stridently, and grinning
> from ear to ear. "One, two, pow!" he chided, smacking
> Jeremy on the back as he skidded toward his desk.
>
> His lanky frame sank into the chair just long enough
> for his shorts-clad bottom to brush the seat. As if
> striking a red-hot coal, he leaped up sprawling onto
> his neighbor's desk.
>
> Erik dropped into his chair. Staring seriously ahead,
> he reached into his desk and silently pulled out a flat
> yellow box. "What do you do with an empty crayon
> box?" he called shrilly, looking at his teacher.

Erik, a second grader, exhibited most of the characteristics associated with hyperactivity. The hyperactive child is usually a male. He is a study in motion. He is in a state of purposeless activity much of the time. He runs, jumps, twists, climbs, touches, pokes, pinches, chatters, and makes mouth noises. He is impulsive. His eyes dart here and there. A slight noise may garner his full but fleeting attention. No toy or activity holds his interest for any length of time. His speech is staccato, rapid, and self-centered. He pursues a topic for a limited time. He interrupts family and classroom discussions with irrelevant comments. He cannot attend long enough to follow ongoing conversation. Even during sleep the hyperactive child is unable to relax. He tosses, turns, twitches, and calls out or moans. He may be so restless that staying covered throughout the night is difficult.

This child does not "act out" to gain attention. His behavior is outside his control. His inability to attend to task results in failure both in the classroom and at home. His impulsive, overactive behavior alienates him from both adults and peers. The result is an unhappy child with a low sense of self-esteem.

There are two types of hyperactivity: primary and secondary. Each stems from a different basis. Before the disorder can be effectively treated, the cause must be identified. This requires both a medical and an educational-psychological evaluation.

Primary Hyperactivity

Primary hyperactivity is physiologically based. It is a medical problem. Only a very small percentage of children exhibiting hyperactive behavior fit this diagnosis. The symptoms may be discernible as early as infancy. The baby is irritable, restless, and difficult to soothe. The behavior becomes more obvious during toddlerhood. The child runs instead of walking. He is prone to accidents because of his impulsiveness and inability to pay attention to what he is doing. He is unable to sit still. He does not respond to your parenting efforts. Attempts by others to control or channel his excessive energy are met with failure.

If you have a hyperactive baby or toddler, you are always tired. You are attuned to his activities both night and day. You feel on call 100 percent of the time. You are constantly concerned for his safety and welfare. Even though you keep household chemicals and medications well out of reach, you know he will find something to put in his mouth. You are afraid to leave him out of your sight for fear he will injure either himself or furnishings in the household.

When the hyperactive child enters school, his problems increase. He is easily distracted and cannot concentrate. He cannot complete assignments or follow classroom discussions. He is disruptive.

Jack, a first grader, was in constant motion. His feet were off the ground as soon as they touched it. He continually touched, pinched, or pulled at other children or their belongings. He persistently talked and made mouth noises. He could not concentrate long enough to complete classroom assignments. His behavior was no less frantic at home.

The medical history revealed that Jack had been a restless sleeper and difficult to console during infancy. As a toddler, he did not respond to his parents efforts to control him. He repeated kindergarten because of "immaturity."

Findings from the medical evaluation showed no abnormalities except hyperactive behavior during the examination. The educational assessment indicated appropriate learning patterns. The psychological workup suggested his behavior problems were a result of his inability to control his level of activity.

The pediatrician recommended a one-week medication trial. The effect was dramatic. Jack's behavior quieted, and he was able to interact appropriately both at home and in school. After the week was up, the medication was stopped. His hyperactive behavior recurred.

Jack was diagnosed as having primary hyperactivity and was treated successfully with medication.

Jack's case is not uncommon. The child with primary hyperactivity is often diagnosed only after a trial of medication treatment has been prescribed. When the physical, psychological, and educational evaluations do not indicate other reasons for the excessive behavior, an assumption can be safely made that a primary nervous system dysfunction is at the base of the disorder. A medication trial confirms or denies the assumption, since medication only affects primary hyperactivity.

Treatment for Primary Hyperactivity

Medication is the most effective treatment for children and adolescents with primary hyperactivity. The available medications which have proved beneficial over many years of experience and study are Ritalin, Dexidrine, and Cylert. Just how these stimulants paradoxically work to calm the patient's behavior is not completely understood. They seem to affect certain nerve cells that control impulsivity, attention span, filtering of unimportant stimuli, and processing of perceptual input. Research on these drugs has found them to be safe and effective when used appropriately. Appropriate usage means using the smallest dose necessary for controlling the hyperactive behavior, never experimenting with the dosage on your own without the guidance of the physician, using the medication only when it is needed and as it is prescribed, and having regular evaluations of the efficacy of the medication on your youngster.

Appropriate use and dosage of medication is determined through careful observation by the physician, parent, teacher, and educational therapist or mental health professional. To assist in accurate observation, behavior scales are completed on your child by you and the classroom teacher prior to the medication trial, during the trial, and after the medication is stopped at the end of the trial. These scales cover activity level, learning style, and social-emotional behavior. Comparisons of his behavior while on and off the medication are made.

If your child does not have primary hyperactivity, the medication may work as a stimulant, and his activity level increases dramatically. This usually happens very shortly after the first dose is taken. If this occurs, the medication is immediately stopped with no harm to the patient. You may wonder how your youngster could be more active than he already is. Believe us; he can! If you have not been properly informed, this increase in behavior can frighten you. Although uncomfortable for both you and your child, the activity increase wears off in about four hours.

When your youngster's overactive behavior is a result of primary hyperactivity, he does not become more stimulated by the medication. The medication either calms him or no difference is seen in his behavior. With either of these results, you and the physician work with the other team members to determine the appropriate dosage needed for his optimal control. This is accomplished through continued medication trials and observation.

Parents of children who have primary hyperactivity are thrilled at the prospects of a calmer child and the opportunity for him to become successful at home and in school; at the same time, they are also concerned about the side effects of medication. Of the available medications, Ritalin is the most commonly used. It comes as both a short-duration and a sustained-release tablet. Let's review the real and mythical side effects of this drug.

The side effects of Ritalin have been widely reported. Some have not been substantiated. The main side effects are: (1) decreased appetite—this is dose-dependent; (2) wakefulness at night—this is seen when a dose is given late in the day; (3) apathy—this is seen when the appropriate dose is exceeded; (4) agitation—this appears when Ritalin is given to a patient who should not be receiving it; (5) tics—this repetitive movement of any muscle is encountered in a very few patients and disappears when the medication is stopped. In some cases, the tics are more disturbing than the hyperactive behavior, and the medication must be discontinued immediately.

Frequently quoted but mythical and unsubstantiated side effects of appropriately used Ritalin include: short stature or an interfering with the attainment of normal height; low blood sugar; liver disease; and psychosis. If Ritalin is properly used, your child will more than likely not show any side effects. All concerns you have regarding the use of medication or its effects should be discussed immediately with your physician.

In determining when your child needs medication, careful observation is the key.

> Melanie had been a pleasant infant and responsive toddler. When she started preschool, her teacher observed that she moved aimlessly around the room, touching whatever she passed. She flitted from activity to activity, not involving herself in any. During rug time, she wiggled, poked other children, and called out.
>
> This purposeless, disruptive behavior continued into kindergarten. Melanie's teacher recommended that the parents seek medical and psychological advice. No physical, thought-processing, or behavioral disorders were found.
>
> A trial of Ritalin was instituted, with a marked decrease in Melanie's disruptive behavior. Withdrawal of the medication resulted in its return.
>
> Ritalin was prescribed for school days only, and Melanie was able to attain success in the classroom.

Some children, like Melanie, are overactive only with the stimulation of group settings. This is called group hyperactivity. Other children, like

Jack, whose story we told earlier, exhibit solo hyperactivity. These children cannot control their behavior either in groups or when they are alone. If a child's behavior is manageable except in groups, medication is generally used only on school days and before stimulating activities like birthday parties. Children and adolescents exhibiting solo hyperactivity may need medication daily. Only a few children require medication seven days a week, 52 weeks a year.

Medication therapy is a route toward success for children who might otherwise be unable to achieve. It works at a physiological level to assist the body in doing what it cannot do by itself. It is not a cure-all, however. Most hyperactive children need counseling and educational assistance as well.

Medication calms a child but it does not change learned behavior patterns. Neither does it magically increase knowledge. Children who have been too active to learn appropriate social behavior or who have been unable to attend in school and learn academically, need the opportunity to develop positive behaviors and learning skills. This is where the services of educational and mental health professionals are needed.

During medication therapy, it is critical that your child be seen regularly by the physician. This ensures that the dose of medication is appropriate and achieving the desired effects, that counseling and/or educational therapy are being pursued as needed, that your child is making academic progress, that there are no signs of unexpected side effects, and that the medication is still needed. Appointments shortly after school begins in September, mid-year, and just before school closes in June are usually adequate.

How is a determination made to stop or continue medication? Stopping medication too soon or continuing its use beyond necessity are not in your child's best interest. Withholding medication one or two times a year and careful observation assures appropriate termination.

With solo hyperactivity, stopping the medication for a trial period during two school vacations and assessing the behavior is effective. For children who have group hyperactivity, the medication must be withheld during school. This is difficult for both your child and his teacher and is usually done only once a year.

Secondary Hyperactivity

Secondary hyperactivity is hyperactivity which is a reaction to a physical, learning, or emotional disorder. It is not the result of neurological malfunctioning, as is found in primary hyperactivity, and does not respond to Ritalin, Dexidrine, or Cylert. Only through an adequate medical, psychological, and educational evaluation can secondary hyperactivity be accurately diagnosed and treated.

Medical Causes of Secondary Hyperactivity

Medical causes of secondary hyperactivity are relatively rare and are usually uncovered during the medical evaluation. Laboratory work may be necessary for accurate diagnosis.

Lucy had been a successful student in elementary and middle school. She had done well during her freshman year of high school.

Shortly after beginning her sophomore year, she became nervous and restless. Her demeanor bordered on hyperactivity. Her grades fell.

A physical examination revealed an enlarged thyroid gland and protruding eyes. Laboratory tests confirmed a diagnosis of hyperthyroidism. Appropriate medical and surgical management brought the thyroid gland under control, and Lucy's behavior returned to her pre-hyperthyroid state.

Hyperthyroidism, cerebral palsy syndrome, epilepsy, and Tourette's disorder are medical conditions which may provoke secondary hyperactivity. Medical intervention, but not the use of medications used to control primary hyperactivity, is required to control the effects.

Allergies and reactions to the ingestion of sugar result in hyperactivity in a small percentage of children. Many parents and teachers believe that most children become "hyper" with sugar. Medical research indicates otherwise. In fact, increased sugar creates lethargy in some children.

In an effort to decrease sugar intake and avoid the possible side effects from sugar substitutes containing saccharine, a common choice is the product NutraSweet, which contains the sweetener aspartame. A very small percentage of children and adolescents develop agitated and uncooperative behavior after ingesting aspartame. Through careful observation, you can determine whether your youngster is affected adversely. Hyperactive behavior resulting from allergies is not easy to diagnose.

> Six-year-old Jane had periods of hyperactive behavior both at home and at school. She had nights of sleep disturbance at random times.
>
> A medical history revealed that Jane had been allergic to cow's milk as an infant. She was taken off dairy products. When she was five, her mother started introducing dairy products back into the diet. No immediate allergic symptoms were noted.
>
> Careful record keeping indicated that Jane's behavior outbursts occurred on days when her dairy intake was greater. Dairy products were once again removed from her diet and the hyperactive behavior and sleep disturbances ceased.

Ferreting out the cause of Jane's hyperactive allergic reactions took time. Once the culprit was detected, dietary management was frustrating but straightforward. When children have a hyperactive response to particular foods or sugar, limiting or avoiding their intake takes care of the problem.

Dietary therapy for children and adolescents who are allergic to food colorings, flavorings, and additives is far more complex. It appears that the common substance in these products is a salicylate-like compound. This type of compound occurs naturally in certain foods as well as artificially in others. Thus, only avoiding the artificial coloring and additives will not do the job. The following is a list of natural foods that also must be avoided to maintain a salicylate-free diet.

Almonds	Currants	Pickles
Apples	Gooseberries	Plums or Prunes
Apricots	Grapes or raisins	Raspberries
Blackberries	Nectarines	Strawberries
Cherries	Oranges	Tomatoes
Cucumbers	Peaches	

Other products which have salicylate compounds (since they contain artificial flavoring and coloring agents) are all medications containing aspirin, most toothpastes, and the vast majority of decongestants, antihistamines, cough medicines, antibiotics, and vitamins.

The magnitude of diet management in this type of allergy is apparent. Results require arduously avoiding the culprit foods and products. Dietary therapy for controlling hyperactive behavior is highly debated among medical professionals. Nonetheless, it is effective in a small but definite group of patients. If your youngster responds to this treatment, by all means pursue it.

Another controversial therapy for handling hyperactivity is nutritional therapy. It involves the use of mega-dose vitamins, trace elements, trace metals, and special amino acids. Research has not consistently shown it to be effective in altering hyperactive behavior.

Traditional allergy treatment is effective in relieving allergic symptoms in some youngsters. Knowledge about allergies and their treatment is expanding. Some allergy patients are helped by avoiding the culprit foods for a period of time, then using a rotation diet. There is evidence that certain holistic health techniques relieve allergic symptoms in some patients. Children whose lives are limited because of allergies may one day have relief and the ability to release their power for success more easily.

Educational and Emotional Causes
of Secondary Hyperactivity

The most common causes of secondary hyperactivity are undiagnosed educational or emotional problems. Educational causes of hyperactivity include low IQ, perceptual disorders, and processing problems.

Eight-year-old Fred was doing poorly in school
both socially and academically. He was disruptive
in class and did not complete assignments. He was
aggressive on the playground.

The medical history revealed that Fred had
been successful in school prior to first grade. He
had been an easy infant and toddler. He was still
cooperative at home unless he was pressed into
doing homework. When pressured, he became
aggressive and belligerent.

During a Dexidrine trial, Fred's behavior grew
worse. A food-additive-free diet was unsuccessful.

The educational evaluation showed that Fred had
severe perceptual problems which interfered with
his ability to succeed in reading and spelling. His
frustration was acted out through disruptive behavior.

Fred qualified for special services through the school.
With the help he needed to succeed, his frustrations
lessened and his behavior improved.

If your youngster has an undiagnosed learning disorder, he is highly
frustrated. He does not understand why he cannot do his classwork as well
as his peers. He tries hard, but his extra effort does not help him do better.
Because he feels "dumb," his self-esteem suffers. His unhappiness and
confusion can result in overactive, disruptive, destructive behavior. The
cycle does not stop here. These children are often mocked, shunned, or
harassed by their peers. This increases their frustration. Children whose
hyperactivity stems from undiagnosed educational disorders need help
badly. Educational therapy and counseling are the usual forms of intervention for these children.

Unresolved emotional conflicts can result in secondary hyperactivity.

Stacy was a 10-year-old fifth grader. She liked
school, did above-average work, and was cooperative
both in school and at home.

Following the Christmas break, she began defying
her teacher and mother, became disruptive in class,
and was hostile and belligerent with her peers.

During a school conference, Stacy's mother was
asked about any situations in the home which might
have disturbed her daughter. She denied any new problems.

A neurological evaluation by the pediatrician and a
psychological assessment by the school counselor did not
pinpoint the problem.

Stacy's mother found a physician who prescribed
medication for Stacy. Her negative behavior increased.

Further evaluation and questioning by the school
psychologist uncovered the fact that Stacy's father, a
long-standing alcoholic, had left home permanently in
December.

Stacy's mother did not lie during the school conference. The father had
moved in and out of the home several times. In her perception, neither the
alcoholism nor the father's final departure were new conditions. She failed
to recognize the impact on Stacy of the father's permanent move.

Stacy's story highlights two important points. First, without a thorough history-taking by the physician, mental health professional, or both,
important details can be overlooked which aid in diagnosis. Second, all
members in a family do not respond to family situations in the same way.
To clarify the responses of the individual in question, all leads must be
followed as completely as possible. Only in this way can accurate
diagnosis and treatment ensue.

Emotional problems which result in secondary hyperactivity require
the services of a mental health professional.

Educational and Psychological Remediation

If your child has been diagnosed as having primary hyperactivity and
is taking medication, the dramatic change in his behavior seems almost
magical. You feel so elated that he has calmed down, it may take you

several days or weeks to recognize that his problems are not cured. Most hyperactive children have learned negative behaviors and habits which must be reshaped. Their academic skills are often weak, since they have been unable to attend either to their teacher or to their classwork. The educational therapist and mental health worker are the team members who will assist your youngster toward releasing his power for educational and emotional success.

If your child has hyperactivity which is secondary to an educational or emotional disorder, remediation is a must. The behavior will change only as the primary problem is treated.

The type of educational remediation you seek for your youngster will depend on the diagnosis. If he has primary hyperactivity without a secondary learning disorder, the assistance of a tutor may be sufficient to help him catch up in his weak academic skills. If the hyperactive behavior is the result of a perceptual, processing, or language disorder, an educational therapist or language specialist will be needed.

Usually the child needing educational assistance has a session with the professional once or twice a week. As well as working on the learning problem, he will learn compensatory skills, such as time management, organization, study aides, and test-taking strategies.

When psychological counseling is recommended, you may feel resistant to the suggestion. You might think you are at fault for your youngster's problem behavior. Some parents feel it is a stigma to receive mental health therapy. If primary hyperactivity is being treated with medication and you have seen behavior changes, you may feel time will take care of any continuing problems. If the educational basis for secondary hyperactivity is being remediated or the emotional stressor causing the hyperactive behavior is transitory, you may think counseling is unnecessary. None of these is the case.

Resisting the professional recommendations you have paid for in both time and money is not in your child's best interest. Often hyperactive children have low self-esteem. They have not usually been successful children by academic measures. Their relationship skills are often poorly developed. They need the guidance of a trained professional to learn how to recognize and understand their feelings, develop social skills, and communicate with others.

Talking and play therapy are techniques used for gaining insights and developing skills. Individual, family, and group therapy are treatment possibilities. You will probably be asked to participate in part of the sessions even when family therapy is not the primary focus. You may also be asked to schedule some appointments for yourself to work through your own feelings about parenting a difficult child and to increase your parenting skills. The therapist will not judge what you have or have not done in the past as a parent. She will assist you in becoming a more effective parent now.

Parenting the Hyperactive Child

Two of the most important parenting skills you can use with your hyperactive child are consistency and follow-through. Consistency means that your youngster can count on you to respond to him in the same or a similar way each time he behaves in a particular way. Let's say, for example, that you have a standard in your home that no snacks are eaten after dinner at night. Your nine-year-old has recently started eating a small portion or none of his evening meal. If you are consistent, he knows that it does not matter whether he eats all or none of his meal, he will not eat again until breakfast. No matter how much he complains about his hunger he can count on you to mean what you say—no snacks after dinner. Consistency results in greater cooperation from your child because he knows what to expect from you. Consistency helps your youngster modify his behavior to fit the family standards.

Follow-through means just what it says. It means following through on what you say you are going to do or on requests you make of your youngster. One of the bits of advice we give the parents who come to us is, "If it's important enough to say the first time, it's important enough to follow through on." How often do you find yourself asking your child to do a particular task three or four times? Most of us fall into that trap. Usually by the fourth or fifth time we ask, the child responds because he hears that special tone in our voice that says, "This time I mean it!" We can create better cooperation in our children if we either mean what we say the first time we say it and assist our youngster to respond at that time or we simply don't say anything until we have time to follow through.

When you are interacting with a youngster who is moving at full speed during all his waking hours, it is difficult to be consistent. You are tired and often angry. It is easier not to deal with problems than to confront them. You may not even know what to confront and what to ignore.

> Mr. and Mrs. North were participating in counseling with their son Ron. For homework, the therapist asked the family to develop a list of house rules.
> During the following session, they presented their list of 20 rules. "I can never do all that," complained 12-year-old Ron.
> "How do you plan to implement these standards?" asked the counselor.
> "We just expect him to follow them," replied Mr. North.

Under the best of conditions, just expecting your child to follow the rules rarely works. With a child who has or has had a control problem, it never works.

In counseling, the Norths learned several hints about developing house rules. First, three or four rules are a reasonable number to focus on at one time. Second, a child is more likely to follow the rules if he actively participates in creating them. Third, if a rule is important enough to have, it is important enough to enforce.

Many families have rules about every aspect of family life. Both parents and children are aware, however, that most of them are ignored much of the time. The youngsters know it is worth the risk of not following an unwanted rule because there is a high chance nothing will happen as a consequence. In other words, the rule is inconsistently enforced.

When reshaping your child's behavior, sit down together and decide three or four areas in which you both want to see change. Create no more than four rules. Write the rules using positive, precise language. Hang them in an easy-to-see place. The refrigerator door works for many families.

This: Jeri will put her clothes in the hamper each
            night before bed.
Not This: Jeri will not leave her clothes on the floor.
                              or
This: Timothy will make his bed each morning before
            breakfast.
Not This: Timothy will not eat breakfast until he has
            made his bed.

You notice that the correctly stated rules are positive. They clearly define the expected behavior. There is not room for misinterpretation which can lead to arguments. Each rule indicates the what, the where, and the when.

In the incorrect examples, the rules are stated in the negative and are open to misinterpretation. Jeri might easily fling her clothes over the back of a chair and, when confronted by her mother, say, "My clothes aren't on the floor." Mother might respond, "You know your dirty clothes go in the hamper, not on the chair." Thus, the arguing begins and the implementing of the standard of putting dirty clothes where they belong is ignored.

If you do not feel you can consistently monitor four rules, create two or three. Your child will begin to follow the house standards when he recognizes that you mean, without question, for them to be followed. As you learn to be consistent, his appropriate behavior will begin to generalize to areas in which you have not made specific rules.

Children want to belong and want to be recognized. Hyperactive children have not had many positive experiences with belonging and recognition. Make sure to support your youngster by acknowledging as many positive steps toward growth as you can.

During a counseling session, Ms. Dickson expressed concern about reinforcing her daughter Lisette.

"If I keep telling her how good she is, won't she become conceited?" asked Ms. Dickson.

The counselor explained that words like "good" and "bad" are judgments. "You are not judging Lisette's behavior when you reinforce and support her," she said. "You are pointing out positive changes and bringing them into Lisette's awareness. You are also expressing appreciation. Instead of saying, 'You were a good girl today,' you might say, 'I like the way you made your bed this morning and brushed your teeth the first time I reminded you.' "

Supportive, reinforcing statements need to be used liberally with your child. They will not result in conceit. They will help him feel good about himself, feel he is contributing positively to the family unit, and recognize that he is a capable human being.

Follow-through is the sister to consistency in reshaping behavior. It is the willingness to let your child experience the consequences of his behavior.

David missed the bus two or three mornings a week. He dawdled over breakfast, couldn't find his book bag, and didn't respond to his mother's prompting.

Each time David missed the bus, his mother drove him to school. She was angry at David and grew angrier as the weeks went by.

"What keeps you from telling David that when he misses the bus he'll need to walk to school?" asked the counselor.

"Well, then he'd be late to school and get in trouble there. Also, he's already behind in his work. He needs to be in class," replied Ms. Haskell.

The counselor assisted Ms. Haskell in recognizing that David's current consequences for missing the bus were positive. David got a ride to school— there was no reason for him to want to catch the bus. Ms. Haskell also learned that by rescuing David, she was not teaching him to be independent and responsible for his choices.

With the counselor's support, Ms. Haskell discussed the situation with David. The consequence for missing the bus was to walk to school. He walked to school twice. Those were the last two times David missed the bus. Too frequently parents do not follow through on established consequences. They feel sorry for their youngster or do not want him to be angry or upset. Sometimes they simply do not want to take the time for this important step in effective parenting.

Your hyperactive child is capable of behaving appropriately with your guidance and support. He wants to be successful. He wants your affection and recognition. Being consistent and following through may feel burdensome. Sometimes they are. The results, however, are well worth the time and effort it takes. Not only will your youngster feel more successful, your relationship with him will change. He will resist you and push you less because he trusts that you mean what you say. As he pushes less, you will like him better.

Prognosis

When your child is diagnosed as being hyperactive, one of the questions you will have is, "Will he always be hyperactive or will he outgrow it?" Twenty years ago it was believed that when hyperactive children entered puberty the hyperactive behavior ceased or dramatically diminished. It is now well-documented that some children with primary hyperactivity carry their disorder into adult life.

Eventually, 85 to 90 percent of primary hyperactive children no longer need medication and function well without it. The remaining 10 to 15 percent benefit from continuing medication during adolescence and adulthood. Without it, these troubled individuals fail at school, jobs, marriage, and social interactions. The same medications used during childhood are used with adolescents and adults. Educational therapy or psychological counseling may be necessary on a regular or intermittent basis.

The belief once prevailed that the medications used to curtail hyperactivity during childhood stimulated such behavior after puberty. These drugs work as stimulants in the general population, but not with patients exhibiting primary hyperactivity, regardless of age. A prominent East

Coast medical journal published a study years ago documenting the same beneficial results to adolescents and adults as seen in younger patients. Since, both further research and observation have corroborated the results.

There are few statistics on hyperactive adults. After leaving the childhood and adolescent care given by the pediatrician, few adults take this problem to a physician. If they seek psychological help, they may fail to let the therapist know they were previously treated for hyperactivity.

As an effective parent, you must let your older adolescent who is on medication for hyperactivity know that the syndrome may persist through adult life. He must relay this information to his future physician and any therapists he works with.

> Mark was a 22-year-old college dropout. He could not hold a job, nor did he have a satisfying social life.
>
> He was diagnosed as having primary hyperactivity in elementary school. He was placed on medication which he continued throughout high school. During high school he was a successful student, a varsity athlete, and enjoyed an active social life.
>
> During a visit to the student health office early in his college career, he was told that Ritalin does not help adults. He stopped the medication. His grades fell, and his social life suffered. Shortly thereafter, he flunked out of school. Afraid to tell his parents, he worked and pretended to go to college. He could not keep a job.
>
> Mark's parents discovered his plight. Counseling was pursued, and a physician was found who prescribed a medication trial. The trial produced the same positive effect as the use of medication had been during high school.

Stopping medication while it is still necessary is devastating for the patient. Once your child leaves home, he must take responsibility for taking care of himself for continued optimal success.

Secondary hyperactivity becomes controlled when the primary learning or emotional disorder is treated. Recurring signs of hyperactivity can clue you to the fact that your youngster is experiencing distress in some area of his life. Discovering and handling the problem are mandatory for his continued achievement.

Check List for Hyperactivity

The following check list includes some of the most common traits of the child with attention deficit disorder with hyperactivity. If you find your child exhibits three or more of these characteristics, discussing his behavior with the pediatrician is warranted.

	Yes	No
1. As an infant, my child was irritable, hard to console, and a poor sleeper.		
2. My child sleeps restlessly or poorly now.		
3. My child engages in purposeless activity at home.		
4. My child engages in purposeless activity at school.		
5. My child is overactive in groups.		
6. My child is overactive when alone.		
7. My child fights and quarrels with playmates.		
8. My child has trouble playing alone with his toys for extended periods.		
9. My child has trouble playing with his toys for extended periods when with other children.		
10. My child does not respond to my parenting.		
11. My child has difficulty paying attention at school.		
12. My child does not finish his classwork.		
13. My child does not finish his homework.		
14. My child does not do his chores.		
15. My child is not liked by other children.		

Check List for Evaluation of Services

The following check list will help you evaluate the services your child is receiving if he has already been diagnosed as exhibiting attention deficit disorder with hyperactivity. If he is not receiving the assistance he needs to release his power for success, speak to the pediatric, educational, or mental health therapist working with him. You may want to take this list with you.

	Yes	No
1. A complete medical evaluation was undertaken.		
2. The following points were discussed: a. Changes have recently occurred in our family (i.e., move, change of school, illness, divorce, death)		
b. My child has or had allergies		
c. Certain foods result in overactivity		
d. A recent change in diet has occurred		
e. I have high expectations for my child		
f. A prior medical evaluation revealed a potential source of hyperactivity		
g. A prior educational-psychological evaluation revealed learning or emotional problems		
3. The physician explained the results of the evaluation in terms I understood.		
4. The physician discussed the results with my child in terms he understood.		
5. An educational evaluation was performed.		
6. The results of the evaluation were explained to me in terms I understood.		
7. The results of the evaluation were explained to my child in terms he understood.		

continued . . .

	Yes	No
8. A psychological evaluation was performed.		
9. The results of the evaluation were explained to me in terms I understood.		
10. The results of the evaluation were explained to my child in terms he understood.		
11. A school observation was done on my child.		
12. If warranted, a medication trial was undertaken.		
13. The educational-psychological therapist observed my child while he was on the medication.		
14. I completed a behavior rating scale prior to and during the medication trial.		
15. The classroom teacher completed a behavior rating form prior to and during the medication trial.		
16. My child is regularly monitored by the physician if he is on medication.		
17. My child has been taken off medication in the past 12 months to evaluate whether it is still needed.		
18. Diet therapy has been discussed with me.		
19. If appropriate, diet therapy has been tried.		
20. My child has been permanently taken off medication or a diet I think he needs.		
21. My child's school performance has improved.		
22. My child's social-emotional behavior has improved.		
23. My child can verbalize at least three ways in which he feels better about his school and social abilities.		

7

The Child with an Attention Deficit Disorder without Hyperactivity

Children who underachieve come in all shapes and sizes. They range in age from beginners in school to those who have nearly finished and are ready to embark into the world of work. Underachievers cover the continuum of behaviors from the most retiring to the child with hyperactivity. Among this wide, wonderful variety of students, one of the most elusive and difficult to detect is the child with an attention deficit disorder without hyperactivity.

Attention deficit disorder without hyperactivity is commonly referred to as ADD or simply attention deficit disorder. We use these labels interchangeably throughout the chapter. ADD is pronounced by each letter name, A-D-D, and not like the word *add*. It is a relatively new diagnosis and refers to a group of children who have the same signs of inattention and impulsivity as the hyperactive child but who do not have and never showed hyperactive tendencies. As you remember from reading chapter 6, hyperactive children show recognizable symptoms of the disorder as early as babyhood and early childhood. The child with ADD is usually not identified until he is school age, and often he has completed several years of school before someone recognizes he needs assistance to release his power for success.

This child is an enigma to his parents, teachers, and all but the most discerning pediatricians, educators, and mental health therapists. Of all the disorders resulting in underachievement, his is the most likely to go undiagnosed or to be misdiagnosed.

Frequently you, the parent, show the first real concern about a child with ADD. Many loving parents who would not think of overtly ridiculing their child have come to us in confusion and exasperation. "I don't know what's wrong with him," they say. "It's like he's from another planet. He's a real space case. I don't know where his mind is, but it's sure not here!" These parents are not being mean or unloving. They are using the most descriptive words they can to depict their child's behavior. It is true; many children with attention deficit disorder do seem to be "someplace else." Not all, though. That is what makes an accurate diagnosis difficult. The symptoms of ADD can be very subtle.

Both in the classroom and in the family, children with ADD can be easily overlooked. They do not cause observable trouble nor are they disruptive. In fact, many do all they can to blend into the classroom or family unit as an unobtrusive entity. At home and in school they go through the motions of completing chores or assigned tasks, while not effectively accomplishing them.

> Jerome, a fifth-grader, sat quietly in the classroom. His teacher was giving instructions for the completion of an assignment. "We have 15 minutes until recess. You may use the time to begin answering the questions at the end of the chapter," she said. "Any that you don't finish you may do for homework."
>
> Jerome looked at the clock. He took his book out of his desk and turned to the questions. He put his name on his paper, erased it, and rewrote it. He thumbed through the chapter looking at the pictures. He put a 1) on the top line of his paper and looked at more pictures. When the class was dismissed for recess, Jerome folded his paper and put it in his book.

Jerome looked like he was hard at work. If his teacher had asked him what he was doing, he would have said he was looking for answers to the questions. That is what he was intending to do and what he thought he was doing. He could not stay focused on reading the text to find the answers, though, because he was distracted by the pictures. A casual glance around the classroom would indicate that Jerome was a student doing his assign-ment. He was sitting quietly at his desk, was using his text, and had some writing on his paper. Only closer observation revealed this was not the case. Teachers and parents are often unaware of how little the child with ADD is accomplishing until they are forced to carefully observe him.

The child with ADD is an unsuccessful student. He is passed from grade to grade, not succeeding yet not failing. He does not make a strong impression on his teachers or peers. He is locked in his own world, unable to release his power for success.

Characteristics of the Child with an Attention Deficit Disorder

The primary characteristics of the child with ADD are inattention and impulsivity. If your child has an attention deficit disorder, you undoubt-edly feel frustrated. His behaviors are annoying. You feel sad that your love for him is not expressed as much as your aggravation at him. Until you understand your youngster's dilemma, it can seem as if his behavior is purposeful. It is not. The child with an attention deficit disorder cannot control his inattentive and impulsive behavior any more than the hyperac-tive child can control his overactivity.

The child with ADD often fails to finish what he starts. It does not matter whether the task is homework or a play activity. His attention wanders. Much of the time he does not seem to listen. It is as if he is daydreaming. He rarely responds the first time you make a request of him, and in conversations his contribution may appear to have nothing to do with the topic. He has difficulty concentrating on his schoolwork or on any task which requires sustained attention. He is easily distracted. In younger children, the inability to attend often comes across as confusion. In older children and adolescents it appears as an attitude of not caring. This is far from true. He is a child who cares and wants to succeed, and his disorder prohibits him from achieving the success he desires.

Many children with ADD are impulsive. They often act before they think. Parents of these impulsive children live with constant anxiety because they fear for their child's safety.

Eight-year-old Joy loved to ride her shiny red bike.
More than anything she wanted to ride it to school.
She knew all the rules for bike riding and could
tell anyone who asked her. She was especially aware
of the rule about walking her bike across the street
and looking both ways before crossing.

Although Joy knew the rules, she did not
consistently follow them. If an adult was with her,
with a reminder, she remembered to look both ways
before crossing the street. When alone, she climbed
off her bike to walk it across and usually started
across without looking. Joy was not aware that she
did not look for traffic.

When confronted about her behavior, she denied it. "I always look both ways," she replied. "Otherwise I might get hit by a car." Her inattention and impulsivity controlled her more than her knowledge of safety rules.

As you can imagine, the child with ADD needs lots of supervision. He also needs more guidance than many children. He has difficulty organizing his work or play activities. This results in frustration and failure. As with his other behaviors, he is not disorganized because he wants to be or because he is rebelling, he simply has a limited capacity to organize effectively. The child shifts excessively from one activity to another without seeming to invest himself in any. He may interrupt conversations or call out in his classroom.

A child with an attention deficit disorder is not easy to parent. Neither is he easy to have in a classroom. You and his teachers are constantly challenged as to how to get through to him. Your attempts to use effective parenting skills often meet with failure, so you feel inadequate. Effective teaching techniques that work with other students do not seem to work with this child. Just as you feel lost, so does he. He does not know why he cannot succeed.

The child with ADD can be helped, and appropriate evaluation and intervention assist him to release his power for success both in the classroom and at home. The team approach is vital in this process.

Just as with hyperactivity, there are two types of attention deficit disorder. One is primary attention deficit and has a physiological basis. The other, secondary attention deficit, is rooted in an educational or psychological problem. To accurately determine the cause of the disorder and prescribe the appropriate treatment, the services of the physician, and of educational and mental health professionals are required.

Primary Attention Deficit Disorder

Primary attention deficit disorder is a medical diagnosis. That is, the root of the inability to attend is physiologically based. The disorder is the result of a dysfunction in the central nervous system. The mechanism in the brain which controls the ability to filter extraneous stimuli and attend to essential stimuli does not work effectively. The area of the brain which is affected is not known, nor is it understood how the mechanism works. Only the results of the malfunction are known and observable: the child cannot pay attention to or complete tasks confronting him.

You are well aware of the initial steps in determining the disorders leading to underachievement. Attention deficit disorder is no different. The first step is the medical evaluation. Next is an educational-psychological evaluation. During the evaluation process, input from the classroom teacher and a school observation are imperative for accurate diagnosis. As you remember in the story of Jerome, only meticulous observation that concentrated entirely on him illuminated the fact that, as busy as he looked, he was not working on task. Both you and the classroom teachers will complete behavior rating scales. These will clarify behavior differences that may exist between home and school.

The usual treatment for children with primary ADD is medication. As in hyperactivity, the drugs of choice are Ritalin or Dexidrine. It is not well-understood how these stimulants work in the child; however, effective results are observable and easily documented.

> Judy was a cheerful, friendly seven-year-old
> who enjoyed school. She was repeating first grade
> because, as a six-year-old, she had been unable to

complete class assignments and had not participated
in classroom activities. No improvement was
seen during her second year as a first-grader.

Upon the request of the teacher, Judy's parents
sought the help of the pediatrician. Nothing abnormal
was found during the medical exam. The doctor
requested a psychological and educational evaluation.
Both indicated Judy was functioning within normal
limits. It was noted she had difficulty attending to task.

The pediatrician advised a seven-day trial on Ritalin
with a re-evaluation by the educational psychologist
while Judy was on medication. During the trial, her
ability to stay on task and complete schoolwork
improved dramatically. When taken off the medication,
her previous lack of attention was observed.

Medication therapy was implemented with Judy,
and she began achieving to her academic potential.

Judy was an interesting case because, aside from her inability to complete her school work, she did not show any other signs of ADD. She was interested in many activities and had no trouble sticking with them. She was alert and interested in her surroundings. She was not a day-dreamer. She was an excellent conversationalist. Her mother referred to her as an "ideal child." It was only during the educational-psychological evaluation and school observation that it was noted that she did not attend to task well. In comparison to many children with ADD, Judy completed a large percentage of her work. Her off-task behaviors included erasing, retracing letters and numbers, and long pauses in her work. Remember, in the beginning of the chapter we stated that children with attention deficit disorder can be easily overlooked? Judy is an excellent example of a child who would have gone undiagnosed without the careful following of the steps we are suggesting for releasing the power for success in underachieving children.

Since the process behind a primary attention deficit disorder is not understood, it is usually only with a medication trial that the physician can diagnose the disorder accurately. When the physical, psychological, and educational evaluations do not reveal other causes for the child's inability to attend, the assumption can be safely made that a dysfunction in the central nervous system is at the base. The medication trial either confirms or denies the assumption, since medication only affects primary ADD. If the child has a primary attention deficit, he will respond to the medication. The medication will allow him to attend to task. Results are immediate.

If the attention deficit is not primary in nature, the prescribed drug works as a stimulant in the child and he becomes temporarily hyperactive. This can be frightening for both you and your youngster if you are not prepared for the possibility. No harm is done to the child, and, since both Ritalin and Dexidrine are short-acting drugs, these negative side effects wear off in about four hours.

When a medication trial is prescribed, both you and the classroom teacher are asked to fill out behavior rating scales prior to, during, and following the trial. A school observation during the trial can be beneficial. When that is not feasible, an appointment with the educational or psychological therapist can suffice.

Occasionally, a child with primary ADD has no response to the medication. This is frustrating to the child, the parents, and the professionals working with the youngster. This child is difficult to accurately diagnose and even more difficult to remediate. Fortunately, the occurrence of this situation is rare.

Children on medication for primary ADD must be followed by the pediatrician at regular intervals. This is necessary to ensure that the dosage is adequate, the behavioral results are appropriate, school progress is satisfactory, and emotional relationships are effective. Your child will be taken off medication for a short period of time at least once every 12 months to assess whether it is still needed. Using medication without follow-up, and assuming or hoping that it will solve the child's problem, is inappropriate.

If you have questions or concerns about the use of medication, refer to the section in chapter 6 on primary hyperactivity. If your questions are still unanswered, do not hesitate to talk to your pediatrician. He will be glad to answer them. At this point we must say that all professionals do not agree that attention deficit disorder without hyperactivity is a specific diagnosis. The use of medication to remediate its effects is controversial. As we said in chapter 5, we are neither proponents nor opponents of medication for controlling disorders resulting in underachievement. Each patient must be carefully evaluated and treatment prescribed on an individual basis. We *do* know that there is a group of children who have a primary attention deficit disorder, and they *do not* respond to educational, psychological, or effective parenting strategies; however, when medication is used in conjunction with these strategies, the child is responsive and achieves success. Medication is not a cure for attention deficit disorder. It is an effective part of treatment for some youngsters.

Secondary Attention Deficit Disorder

Secondary ADD is the inability to stay on task due to the presence of a disease or disorder other than primary nervous-system dysfunction. It does not respond to Ritalin or Dexidrine. The syndrome is a result of a learning, emotional, or physical disorder. Some specific causes are learning disability, low IQ, emotional problems with depression or withdrawal, impaired vision or hearing, low thyroid function, epilepsy, and allergies. Accurate diagnosis of secondary ADD depends on the medical and educational-psychological evaluations.

Medical Causes of Secondary Attention Deficit Disorder

During the medical evaluation, organic causes of secondary ADD are ruled out or confirmed. If vision or hearing loss, epilepsy, or low thyroid function are suspected, appropriate medical procedures are implemented.

Peter was a quiet six-year-old whose classroom behavior and academic abilities were inconsistent. Sometimes he was attentive and sharp. At other times, he stared into space as if in a daydream. At home his parents noted frequent spells of staring.

Both medical and educational-psychological evaluations were undertaken and Peter was found to be normal. The physician prescribed a trial of Dexidrine. This resulted in aggressive, hyperactive behavior. Medication was discontinued. No further evaluation was pursued, and the parents assumed Peter would outgrow his daydreaming.

Peter repeated first grade with no changes in his behavior or academic success. His teacher advised the parents to seek a second medical opinion about his staring spells. An EEG was done as a result of the medical history. The test revealed a form of petite mal epilepsy. Appropriate medication, but not those used to treat primary ADD, was started, the staring spells ceased, and Peter excelled academically.

You may wonder why the petite mal epilepsy was not diagnosed initially. All professionals are fallible. Perhaps the pediatrician Peter saw originally was not strongly acquainted with attention deficit disorder and its possible causes. Perhaps he believed that Peter's problem was one of immaturity. Most physicians do not prescribe laboratory work unless it is strongly warranted. In his estimation, Peter's symptoms did not warrant laboratory tests. For most problems resulting in underachievement, lack of immediate diagnosis simply means lost time, time during which the child could be releasing his power for success and achieving. Fortunately for Peter, a perceptive teacher and the willingness of his parents to pursue the cause of his staring spells and lack of academic achievement resulted in accurate diagnosis and treatment of his problem.

When the medical findings for a child's inability to attend to task are negative, the services of the mental health professional and educational therapist are recommended. An educational and psychological evaluation sheds light on emotional and learning factors contributing to the problem.

Emotional and Learning Causes of Secondary Attention Deficit Disorder

Emotional and learning causes for secondary ADD are more prevalent than medical causes. Learning culprits are learning disability and low IQ. A thorough educational evaluation reveals whether a learning problem is at the root of the child's inability to attend, and, if so, points the way toward effective treatment.

> Seven-year-old Richard, a second-grader, rarely was aware of what was happening in class. Although he looked at his teacher when she talked, he could not answer questions when she called on him. He completed assignments only when someone sat next to him and guided him through the tasks.
> A medical workup revealed no abnormal findings. During the educational and psychological evaluation, the evaluator discovered that Richard had difficulty understanding the instructions she gave him. The results of the assessment indicated that Richard had a severe auditory perceptual disorder. He could hear well, but his brain could not process the information in a usable way.

Richard's disorder made it difficult for him to achieve in the classroom because he could not understand what he was supposed to do. No medication or maturity would alleviate his problem. The diagnosis required educational therapy for Richard and parent education for his parents so they could effectively work with him at home.

Some children with emotional problems show symptoms of secondary attention deficit disorder. Although parents find it hard to understand and accept, children can and do experience emotional problems. When a child is emotionally upset, he cannot concentrate on his school work or on any other task which requires his sustained concentration.

Katie was nine years old, gifted, and attended an ungraded private school. During what was equivalent to her fourth-grade year, she became withdrawn and lost interest in school. She no longer played with the children during recess or lunch hour, complained of stomach upsets and headaches, and rarely finished her classwork. At home she spent most of her time in her room resting because she was tired and did not feel well.

Katie's parents were alarmed at her behavior and symptoms and took her to their pediatrician. He found no physical cause for her fatigue or stomachaches and headaches. He referred the family to a psychologist, whose evaluation revealed that Katie was very angry at her mother and "hated" her sister. She felt guilty for having these feelings. Her inability to express her anger, either by talking to her parents or by acting out, resulted in symptoms associated with depression.

Katie began treatment with the psychologist which included both play and talking therapy. Some sessions involving Katie's family were incorporated into the treatment program. When she began to feel comfortable with her feelings and more secure in her family, her physical symptoms ceased, and she began achieving at school both academically and socially.

Ferreting out the cause of and treating attention deficit disorder can be time consuming. It takes courage to persist. However, your willingness to continue the process by taking the appropriate steps and being a knowledgeable consumer result in the possibility for your child to release his power for success and become an effective student.

Remediation for the Child with an Attention Deficit Disorder

Whether your youngster exhibits primary or secondary attention deficit disorder, educational remediation, counseling, or both can be necessary in assisting him toward releasing his power for success. Academically, he is probably working below grade level because he has not been attentive to classroom activities and assignments. His inability to stick with tasks both at home and at school has resulted in few situations where he has been truly successful. Such lack of success leads to poor self-esteem and a belief that achievement is not possible.

If your child has a primary attention deficit disorder and is on medication, you may be surprised that although he is now capable of following through on the tasks at hand, he does not. Much of a person's behavior is habitual. Whether we know a different way or not, our initial response in situations is usually the one we are used to using. This is no different for a child whose attention deficit is under control. Although your youngster is now able to attend to his studies in class, he may still dawdle over homework or household chores. These learned behaviors need to be reshaped so that more effective habit patterns are formed. Occasionally when children begin medication, their academic achievement and social-emotional behavior improves as if by magic. This is what happened with Susan, whose story you read earlier. These children are the ones whose self-esteem has remained strongly intact because of successes outside the classroom and because of particularly strong and loving support systems. With most children, remediation is necessary.

If your child has a secondary attention deficit disorder, remediation is virtually a must. If the syndrome is the result of a learning or emotional disorder, it is mandatory. The diagnosis gives professionals a guide for the steps to take in assisting him toward achievement. Your willingness to participate with your youngster in the remedial process is the determiner of future success. The process is usually slower than for children with primary ADD, yet persistence yields results.

As parents, you have learned to interact with your inattentive, impulsive youngster in particular ways. You remind him numerous times about his chores. You sit with him to make sure his homework is completed. You lower your expectations for him, since you know he cannot achieve as well as other children his age. It is necessary for you to become aware of these patterns and learn more effective ways of parenting so that you are reinforcing his new abilities.

Educational Remediation

The classroom teacher and educational therapist or tutor are the primary team members participating in your child's educational remediation. Each teacher and therapist has her own particular way of assisting children with special needs to release their power for success. You can ask the classroom teacher how she is meeting your youngster's individual needs. A private professional should let you know on a regular basis what she is doing and how your son or daughter is responding. If she does not, ask.

In the classroom it is important for the child to sit near the front of the room. This is where he is closest to the vital action. The chalkboard is usually at the front of the class, and many teachers stay near the front of the room when giving instructions and leading lessons. When this is where your youngster sits, the teacher can remain more aware of his on-task behavior. Finally, there are fewer distractions at the front of the room, since most of the class sits behind him.

In guiding a child toward appropriate classroom behavior and assignment completion, a reinforcement system is valuable. A 5x7 card taped to his desk, on which he can accumulate positive checks for effective student behavior, is easy for the teacher and highly visible to the child. At the same time, it does not readily draw attention from other students.

> Allison sat in the first row of desks nearest the chalkboard. On the top of her desk was taped an index card marked off in columns corresponding to each hour of the school day.
> During the day, Ms. Cameron, the teacher, put checks on Allison's card when she was working on task. At the end of the day Allison counted her checks and recorded them on the bottom of her card. When she accumulated 100 checks, she and a friend were going to stay after school and do a special project with Ms. Cameron.

Ms. Cameron was assisting Allison in becoming aware of her on-task behavior. She and Allison had worked together to make the check cards and plan the reward. Because Allison loved Ms. Cameron, she was working hard to stay on task and earn special time with her. Including a child in creating his reward system and choosing the reward ensures a greater degree of success.

Immediate feedback is important for most students. It is vital to the success of children with ADD. They need acknowledgment for classwork completed on time, homework turned in on time, and accuracy of work. These are children who have had little success in these areas. Recognizing them for their effort in becoming successful students makes the time and energy they spend worthwhile. Before they can become self-motivated to achieve, they need the recognition of others.

Tutoring or educational therapy will probably be necessary in aiding your child toward grade-level work. If the attention deficit disorder is primary, tutoring in deficient subjects can often remediate the problem. If a learning disorder is the cause of the attention deficit, therapy by a person trained to work with learning disabilities is required. The educational evaluation provides the data necessary in preparing an effective remedial program. Techniques used with learning disabled students are incorporated. These procedures are described in chapter 8.

Social and Emotional Remediation

The physician, educational evaluator, or mental health professional may recommend counseling for your child and you. Children with ADD have experienced lack of success both academically and in the home. Many have had less than successful experiences socially. Because of their "spacy" behavior, sometimes other children think they are "weird." It is not at all uncommon for these children to report that the kids at school "say I'm weird," or "call me weirdo." Since children with an attention deficit are not clearly aware of what is happening in their environment, your child may not know the skills necessary for making or being a friend. A counselor can assist him toward social success and success in the family.

Lack of self-esteem, depression, and anxiety are common emotional problems needing attention. Through talking and play therapy the mental health professional assists your youngster toward a stronger sense of self.

She teaches him ways of expressing his feelings of sadness, anger, and frustration so that he does not turn them inward and experience depression. She teaches him how to recognize his uptight, anxious feelings and how to practice relaxation techniques that he can use at home and at school to relieve his tension.

If your child is responsive to medication, the successes he begins to experience with his greater ability to carry through on tasks will probably affect his self-esteem in positive ways. Some children, however, become anxious about their successes. They know both parents and teachers have higher expectations for them. They fear that they may not meet those expectations, but they also fear that when they do, the expectations will be raised even higher. A counselor can help children experiencing fears of success to understand them and deal with them in positive ways.

Parent education is useful for expanding your repertoire of parenting skills. A counselor can help you set realistic goals with your child. She can assist you in learning to recognize small increments of change to reinforce and support. She can facilitate the development and expansion of your communication skills.

It is difficult to see objectively your own behavior patterns with your child. A counselor can be a mirror and reflect the ways in which you interact and communicate with him. As your child grows and changes, you, too, will want to grow and change. Mental health professionals and parent education classes are excellent resources.

Parenting the Child with an Attention Deficit Disorder

When you live with a youngster who often is not quite "with it," you develop parenting strategies which appear to provide him with some successes. You want so much for him to experience success that you end up rescuing him and manipulating situations for him.

> Debra was 11 years old. She rarely finished
> her classwork. Her teacher required her to take the
> incomplete assignments home as homework.

Most afternoons and evenings Debra worked
four or five hours on her homework and still did not
complete it.

Mrs. Rand, Debra's mother, wanted to help her
daughter succeed. She began doing part of the
homework, and Debra recopied it. In explaining her
intervening she said, "Debra knows how to do the
work. She just can't concentrate long enough to
get it done. When I help her, she finishes it and has
time for some leisure activities."

Mrs. Rand felt sorry for Debra. She loved her daughter and believed
she was creating a way for her to feel successful. In fact, Debra did not feel
successful. She felt guilty. She was not learning to complete tasks on her
own, and felt that, if it were not for her mother, she would be a failure.

In assisting your youngster with his homework, help him break tasks
down into manageable units. Give him the opportunity to work on these
units independently and check with you for validation and support.

During counseling, Mrs. Rand learned to
effectively cooperate with Debra on the homework problem. Each afternoon Debra organized her homework into the order in which she
wanted to do the assignments. She set a timer
for 15 minutes. She worked on an assignment
until the timer buzzed, then went to show her mother
how much she'd progressed. During a five-
minute break after each 15 minutes, she visited
her mom, got a drink of water, or had a mini-
snack. She then returned to work for 15 more
minutes.

Mrs. Rand acknowledged Debra for the work
she completed. She did not intervene in the work
process itself. If Debra had particular problems with
an assignment, they were discussed prior to beginning
or after a 15-minute work segment.

> In time, Debra was able to complete her homework
> in less than half the time it had taken her previously.

Learning to trust that a new or different routine will work takes courage. It is not easy to step back from your child and believe that he can succeed, particularly if he has had a life filled with few successes. Helping him structure for success, then allowing him to do by himself whatever the task may be, contributes to his growth toward independence. He becomes aware of his abilities and develops positive feelings about himself.

When making a request of your child or giving him instructions, have eye contact with him. He is far more likely to listen than if you call to him from another room or try to talk to him while he is doing something else. Ask him to repeat his understanding of what you requested or said. In this way you know if he has accurately processed the information.

Even if your youngster seems to understand what is expected of him, he may not follow through. As an effective parent, it is your job to make sure he does. Both you and he must learn that you mean what you say.

> Allen's job was to empty each of the four waste-
> baskets in his home every other day. If he forgot or
> did only a partial job, his mother did the task.
> In working with a family counselor, Allen's
> mother learned to reinforce partial success and follow
> through with her requests to Allen. When Allen only
> dumped two baskets of trash she said, "Thank you for
> emptying the kitchen and bathroom trash. Now I want
> you to empty the bedroom waste baskets."

Initially Allen was angry that his mother was "making" him do his chore correctly. He was used to getting by with less. Before long, he recognized that his mother was not going to do his chores for him. He learned to trust that she meant what she said.

Assisting your youngster in structuring tasks, supporting each increment in his success, using eye contact when communicating with him, and following through on what you say are highly effective parenting skills. When you use them consistently they give the positive and loving message that you have faith in his ability to succeed. They lead to the creation of a stronger relationship between the two of you, and they guide him toward successful independence.

Prognosis

No long-term studies of children with ADD exist to provide information about their prognosis. It is believed that all children do not outgrow the disorder. Perhaps, since they are not disruptive or belligerent, untreated patients blend into society as adult underachievers who get by in jobs requiring minimal concentration. They learn coping strategies to handle their lives.

Children with either primary or secondary ADD who are accurately diagnosed and treated have an excellent opportunity for success during each stage of their lives if treatment is not prematurely terminated and is resumed throughout life when necessary.

As with any physical, learning, or emotional problem, the child with an attention deficit disorder is far more like other children than he is different from them. If you remember this while taking the steps to care for his special needs, he cannot help growing toward achievement and success.

Check List for Attention Deficit Disorder

The following check list includes some of the most common traits of the child with an attention deficit disorder without hyperactivity. If you find that your child exhibits three or more of these traits, discussing his behavior with the pediatrician is warranted.

	Yes	No
1. My child daydreams more than I think he should.		
2. My child rarely responds the first time I make a request of him.		
3. My child appears to pay attention when I talk to him or ask him to do a task but really has no idea what I've said.		
4. My child has difficulty completing tasks.		
5. Midway through a task, my child seems to forget what he is doing.		
6. My child is forgetful (i.e., forgets his home work, his lunch, does not remember where he puts things).		
7. My child does not play attentively with his toys.		
8. My child watches TV more than I think he should.		
9. My child complains of boredom.		
10. My child is easily distracted.		
11. My child has a difficult time finishing his homework.		
12. My child has a difficult time finishing his classwork.		
13. My child seems confused about what is expected of him.		

continued . . .

	Yes	No
14. My child seems to act before he thinks.		
15. My child knows but does not follow safety rules.		
16. My child interrupts instead of waiting his turn to speak.		
17. My child does not have successful social relationships.		
18. My child says his classmates think he's "weird."		
19. My child seems socially immature for his age.		

Check List for Evaluation of Services

The following check list will help you evaluate the services your child is receiving if he has already been diagnosed as having an attention deficit disorder without hyperactivity. If he is not receiving the assistance he needs to release his power for success, speak to the pediatrician and the educational or mental health therapist working with him. You may wish to take this list with you.

	Yes	No
1. A complete medical evaluation was undertaken.		
2. The following points were discussed: a. Changes have recently occurred in our family (i.e., move, change of school, illness, divorce, death)		
b. My child has or had allergies		
c. I have high expectations for my child		
d. A prior medical evaluation revealed a potential source of attention deficit disorder		
e. A prior educational-psychological evaluation revealed learning or emotional problems		
3. The physician explained the results of the evaluation in terms I understood.		
4. The physician discussed the results with my child in terms he understood.		
5. An educational evaluation was performed.		
6. The results of the evaluation were explained to me in terms I understood.		
7. The results of the evaluation were explained to my child in terms he understood.		
8. A psychological evaluation was performed.		
continued . . .		

	Yes	No
9. The results of the evaluation were explained to me in terms I understood.		
10. The results of the evaluation were explained to my child in terms he understood.		
11. A school observation was done on my child.		
12. If warranted, a medication trial was undertaken.		
13. The educational-psychological therapist observed my child while he was on the medication.		
14. I completed a behavior rating scale prior to and during the medication trial.		
15. The classroom teacher completed a behavior rating scale prior to and during the medication trial.		
16. My child has been taken off medication at least once in the past 12 months to evaluate whether it is still needed.		
17. My child has been permanently taken off medication I think he needs.		
18. My child's school performance has improved.		
19. My child's social-emotional behavior has improved.		
20. My child can verbalize three ways in which he feels better about his school and social abilities.		

8

The Child with a Learning Disability

One of the ways we gain empathy and compassion for someone who is experiencing a problem is to think about a time when we were in a similar situation. The more clearly we remember the details of what we were doing and recall the feelings we had, the better we can understand the person in our lives who is having difficulty. When we reach understanding, we are less likely to judge the way he is handling his problems. Too frequently we do not take time to put ourselves into a position of understanding. We react emotionally to the person in trouble. Interestingly enough, it is often with those who are dearest to us that we respond the most harshly.

As parents, many of us have forgotten what it was like being a child. Oh, if we sit down and reminisce we remember, but moment by moment we do not carry the images or feelings of childhood with us. Unless we make a conscious effort, we may not even be able to relate the feelings we have as adults to those our youngsters experience. When our children are happy and successful, it is easy to love them and express warmth toward them. When they are unsuccessful, it is not unusual to feel disappointment, anger or confusion. Instead of taking a minute to recognize how our offspring is feeling with his lack of success, we react from our own feelings. With disappointment, anger, or confusion, the most common responses are either to pull away from or lash out at the one we think is causing our discomfort. We do this in the crucial time when this child of ours needs our most loving support and guidance.

The child with a learning disability does not experience success regularly. School is hard for him, social relationships often are unrewarding, and he may feel insecure with you because he thinks he is disappointing you. At home, in school, and in extracurricular activities, adults interacting with him give the message, "Why don't you try harder? You could do better if you'd just try." More than likely he cannot try harder. His learning disability prohibits him from releasing his power for success.

Most of you have seen or heard the term *learning disability*. During the past several years, stories and informative articles about the disorder have appeared in popular magazines. Public and commercial television stations have carried programs about the "hidden handicap." Perhaps while you were seeing one of these programs or reading an article you began to think about your own child's underachievement. Something you saw or read sparked a light of recognition. Maybe it was what you learned from the media that encouraged you to pursue an evaluation to discover why your son or daughter was not learning.

When an evaluation indicates that your child has a learning disability, you are filled with questions. What does that mean? Can it be cured? Will he have to go to special classes or a special school? What caused it? Will he ever be able to learn? These are important questions. Some have fairly clear-cut answers. For others the answers are vague and provoke more questions. The term learning disabilities is applied to a field in which even the experts do not agree on the definition, the cause, or the recommended treatment.

Of all the disorders leading to underachievement, learning disability may be the most confusing and frustrating for parents to understand. Nonetheless, since the early 1970s when the label came into vogue, much has been learned about the disorder. In this chapter, we will share the current understandings about this strange malady.

What Is a Learning Disability?

Over the past two decades, what is now called learning disability has gone by various other names: minimal brain damage, minimal cerebral dysfunction, neurological dysfunction, dyslexia, and perceptual difficulties. The terms allude to the fact that something is not working normally in the brain. They are labels. They do not help parents and professionals to understand the child nor do they provide clues as to how to help him.

During the late 1970s, the federal government defined the term learning disability in PL 94–142. We talked about this law in chapter 4 in relation to services for children with special learning needs. This comprehensive law also defined who these special-needs children are. This is how it defines learning disability:

> "Specific learning disability means a disorder in one or more of the basic psychological processes involved in understanding or in using language, spoken or written, which may manifest itself in an imperfect ability to listen, think, speak, read, write, spell, or to do mathematical calculations. The term includes such conditions as perceptual handicaps, brain injury, minimal brain dysfunction, dyslexia, and developmental aphasia. The term does not include children who have learning problems which are primarily the result of visual, hearing or motor handicaps, of mental retardation, of emotional disturbance or of environmental, cultural, or economic disadvantage."

Although the language in the law is not easy to understand, we think it is important for you to see how the learning disability your child has is legally defined, since that definition serves as the guide for both identifying him and providing educational services for him. Let's look carefully at the definition. It says that there is not one single, simple learning disability, but many. It explains that the disorder involves processing problems in speaking, listening, writing, spelling, reading, and arithmetic. In everyday language that means that there is some kind of short circuit in the brain that makes it impossible for your child to either accurately receive information from the environment or express information in a way that shows he can effectively use what he may know. The definition indicates that perceptual difficulties may exist. This means that although your youngster has adequate sight and hearing acuity, he does not understand what he hears and sees in a way that is usable for academic success.

This explicit definition does more than tell us who the learning-disabled are; it also tells us who they are not. They are not people who are blind, deaf, physically disabled, retarded, or emotionally disturbed. They are not children who are educationally disadvantaged as a result of cultural, environmental, or economic factors. In other words, children who are not learning because they speak no English, have inadequate housing, are undernourished, are not exposed to books outside of school, or live in financially disadvantaged families are not learning-disabled.

Some children have multiple disabilities. For example, a visually impaired or emotionally disturbed youth can also have a learning disability. Only when the learning disability is the key reason why the child is not academically successful is it considered the primary diagnosis.

A learning disability is a processing problem. Information from the environment is received through the senses, primarily through sight, hearing, and touch. When a learning disability is present, the information is transmitted to the brain accurately through the sense organs but gets scrambled as it is being processed by the brain. The brain may not organize information in a useful way or store it in forms that can be retrieved from memory. If the received information requires a response and the data has been garbled, the output or response, whether it be a verbal answer or physical action, will be inappropriate.

> Kenny had a visual sequencing problem that
> interfered with his ability to read and spell. He
> could not read or write letters in their correct order.
> No matter how hard he studied, he always missed
> words on the weekly written spelling test.
>
> He spelled the words correctly when his mother
> asked him to spell them to her orally. Frequently,
> he misspelled the words when writing spelling
> sentences. "I don't understand it. He can't even
> copy the words correctly," said Kenny's mother.
>
> Kenny, his parents, and his teacher were frustrated.
> Words that Kenny had known for years had errors.
> *School* appeared as *shcool* and *proof* as *poofr*.

Kenny's misspellings were not a result of lack of effort. Neither were they caused by carelessness or poor study habits. They were a result of his learning disability. Even though he knew how to spell *school* and *proof,* he could not get them down on paper correctly nor could he recognize his errors. The short circuit or processing difficulty in his brain caused him to be unable to see his errors.

No one knows how many different learning disabilities there are. It has been indicated that there may be as many as 100 types. Whatever the actual number, they are usually categorized into five major groups: disabilities of speech and spoken language, written language, reading, and math; and mixed disabilities. A mixed disability is when there is a similar amount of impairment in more than one area.

Within each of these major areas of disability, there are numerous identified problems. Some pertain to the physical body, appearing as a child's difficulty with movement, his speed and dexterity, and his awareness of his body in space. Others relate to a youngster's understanding of time, his use of directionality, and his organizational skills. Still others include the ability to concentrate and the use of short- and long-term memory. Some children, like Kenny in the story above, have problems in sequencing material. Others cannot understand abstract concepts. These are but a few of the many problems which fall into the category of learning disability.

Sometimes in discussions about learning disabilities you have heard the word *dyslexia.* Dyslexia is a term which is no longer widely used among psychological and educational professionals, although it is still used in the medical profession. It refers to a disability in reading and in receiving and expressing language. Other words which you may have heard, although not currently used with regularity, are *dysgraphia* and *dyscalculia.* Dysgraphia means a disability in written language, and dyscalculia refers to a disability in math.

Who Are the Learning-disabled?

Learning disabilities are not rare. Some experts believe that up to 20 percent of the population is affected by some form of the disorder. Disabilities range from mild to severe and from minimally affecting a person's life to plaguing him with social and emotional pain.

Many people with learning disabilities are not even aware that they have them. Probably most of us have minimal disabilities and attribute our actions to some other cause. For example, if our child falls, bumps into furniture, and drops things, we say he is clumsy. When our friend uses her hands or turns her body when giving directions and laughs because she says "right" when she means "left" we think she is overly expressive and scattered. In fact, our youngster may not perceive his body in space well, and our friend may have a problem with directionality!

Early theorists in the field of learning believed that a learning disability was primarily an academically related disorder. Learning-disabled or LD children, as they are commonly called, were not identified until the primary grades, and it was believed that most would outgrow their problems during adolescence. We now know that this is not true. There are warning signals long before children enter school that they may be at risk, and learning-disabled children often grow up into learning-disabled adults.

The learning-disabled are intelligent. They have at least average and often above average to superior IQs. The LD child may feel dumb and appear not to have the capacity to learn; however, his testing profile is very different from that of a youngster who is retarded.

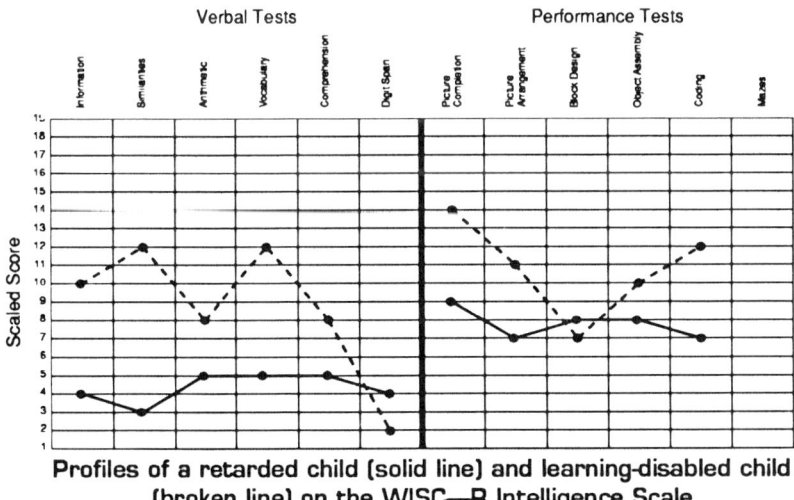

Profiles of a retarded child (solid line) and learning-disabled child (broken line) on the WISC—R Intelligence Scale

A retarded child has what is called a flat profile. He has below average intellectual functioning on each subtest of the intelligence scale and corresponding academic skills. The LD child has a testing profile of peaks and valleys. There is a wide variation in his abilities as measured by the intelligence test. He may test above average to superior in some areas and below average in others. He does not possess equal or similar skills in all academic areas, and his skills are not as strong as his IQ indicates they should be.

Children with learning disabilities are often creative. They seem to see the world in a different way. Since they learn differently, they approach problems differently and often come up with unique solutions.

More boys than girls are learning-disabled. Perhaps as many as three out of every four LD children are males. Currently, reasons for this sex difference are not clear. Genetic and neurological factors are generally considered as the base.

What Causes Learning Disabilities?

By now you may be thinking, "Okay, all this is interesting, but I want to know what caused Bobby's learning disability." That's a tough question. No one knows for certain. Although the experts have some good ideas, most are not proven. What is known is that all learning disabilities do not stem from the same cause. One child might be disabled because of an intrauterine viral infection, another because of oxygen deprivation during or shortly after birth. Prematurity, birth injuries, and birth traumas are associated with the disorder. Severe head injury is believed to be a possible culprit.

Learning disability may be inherited. There is considerable evidence that some LD children come from families in which other members have or had learning problems.

Current researchers are studying the effects of nutrition and food additives on brain functioning in relation to learning disability. It has already been confirmed that some food additives lead to or exacerbate hyperactivity in certain individuals. Perhaps they also affect learning styles.

Through a person's verbal, written, and nonverbal behavior we can see the results or output of a brain that functions differently from what we call normal. Structural differences in the brain can only be proven, however, after an autopsy has been performed following a person's death. There have been studies done on the brains of deceased individuals who had been labeled dyslexic. Information derived from these autopsies indicates that there were subtle cell-structure differences at both the subcortical and cortical levels. This is valuable and interesting information, but it still does not answer the questions, "Why did this happen?" and "What role did it play in the individual's learning problem?"

So little is understood about the causes of the disorder, that it is not wise to spend valuable time and money trying to determine what might have caused your child's disability. Blaming a spouse, a doctor, or an event does not change his problem. It does not help him learn better in school or feel better about himself. What is useful and necessary is following the steps which will help him release his power for success so he can manage his disability and grow toward his academic, social, and emotional potential.

Common Behavior Patterns of Children with a Learning Disability

One of the most puzzling aspects of the LD child is the inconsistency in or unpredictability of his abilities.

"I know all my 5s by memory," said Renae, beaming as she entered the office. "Great!" responded the educational therapist. Renae had been working on her times tables for weeks. She had learned the 2s well and knew most of the 3s and 4s. "Get the stopwatch and flashcards, and let's give it a try." Renae loved playing Beat the Clock with her math facts. Sure enough, she knew her 5s. She whipped the facts off quickly and accurately.

"Now let's mix the 2s, 3s, and 4s with the 5s and play Draw-a-Card," the therapist suggested. They mixed the cards and laid them face down on the table. They took turns drawing a card, reading

the fact, and giving the answer. Renae knew her
5s perfectly and her 3s and 4s moderately well.
She did not know one of the 2s, including 2x5!

Renae's inability to remember material she previously had known well
is not uncommon for LD students. Sometimes the information simply
seems to slip away. The lapse may be temporary. In the next day or two
the skill might be available for use again. Sometimes, however, it must be
relearned as if it never had been known.

Imagine the frustration your child must feel being faced with such a
dilemma. "I know that. I just can't remember it," is his common cry. He
feels ashamed and fearful. Maybe they think I'm not trying, he thinks.
What if they get mad at me? "They" almost always refers to both his
teacher and you. You and the teacher also feel frustrated, afraid, and
overwhelmed. Frequently, these feelings are expressed as anger toward
your youngster.

Often the LD child is impulsive. "Why doesn't he just stop and think
before barging into something," many parents lament. Indeed, it often
seems that acting comes first.

Ms. Anderson's class was studying the months of
the year. The group sat in a circle playing a before-
and-after game.
"Who knows what month comes after..."
began Ms. Anderson.
"I know. I know. It's February!" yelled Ricky.
Ms. Anderson ignored him. "...after April?"
she continued.
"Ohhhh," groaned Ricky. "I thought you
were gonna say January."

Sometimes this impulsive behavior drives you crazy. You want to
shake your child and say, "Just stop, look, and listen. Don't be in such a
hurry. If you'd slow down you'd do better." Sometimes the impulsivity
scares you. "Donny has so many accidents. He just doesn't consider the
risks he's taking." The impulsive child may or may not be aware of the

consequences of his behavior. Even when he can verbalize them, he does not always act in accordance with them. He acts in the moment without thought or fear of the future.

Some learning-disabled children are hyperactive and distractible. They are always running in high gear and rarely stop from the time they wake up until they fall asleep at night. They may even toss, turn, and twitch during sleep. They cannot stay still long enough to concentrate on a task, whether it be reading or building a model plane.

Another LD child may exhibit an attention deficit disorder without hyperactivity. Unlike the hyperactive child, he can settle his body down but not his mind. He cannot attend to the task at hand. The ticking of the clock, the children playing at recess on the other side of the school, and the traffic on the highway, all pull him away from his classwork. He cannot concentrate. His attention span is short. Sometimes parents say, "He just seems to be in outer space." Others say, "I know he could concentrate if he tried. He watches TV for hours on end without moving." Some children do have the ability to attend to tasks they enjoy. Many, however, do not attend as carefully as it appears.

> Tim was watching the Saturday morning cartoons.
> His father walked through the living room, whistling.
> Tim glanced at his dad without saying a word.
> He noticed a piece of lint on the rug next to his knee,
> picked it up, rolled it into a little ball, and tossed it
> back down. He focused on the TV screen for several
> minutes then looked at the scab on his ankle and
> began scratching at it.

Since Tim was sitting quietly, it appeared that he was attending to the television program. Careful observation indicated that he was not. Tim was not doing a task which required careful concentration, so his inability to pay attention did not get in his way. Had he been in the classroom or doing his homework, the distractions he experienced would have interfered with his success.

Some children with learning disabilities are hypoactive or quiet and aloof. They pull into themselves and become lost to the classroom or family. These children rarely cause problems for teachers or parents and easily become overlooked. "He's so much easier to handle than his brother, I guess we just never noticed he was having problems," commented one parent sheepishly.

You may think your child is immature or too dependent. Perhaps he relies on you or on a brother or sister to do tasks for him that he is capable of doing himself. The LD child does not trust his abilities. Too often things do not work out for him. His fear of failure can make him unwilling to attempt new and different activities or even the most familiar jobs.

Many learning-disabled children are rigid in their thinking and in their behavior. They are unaware of the many choices available to them in life and of the endless numbers of ways in which situations can be approached and handled. Their mental flexibility or ability to shift gears in thinking is not well developed. This poses a problem for them in their social relationships and academically.

You may have experienced this rigidity when working with your child on a homework assignment.

> Nancy was writing the summary for her class project. The assignment was to write a two-page paper describing what she had done, why she had chosen to do it, and what she had learned from the project. Upon completing the paper, she asked her mother to read it.
>
> The paper covered the topics but was not organized in paragraph form. When Nancy's mother pointed this out to her, Nancy replied, "My teacher didn't say we had to write it in paragraphs. She just said we had to write a two-page paper."

Nothing her mother said could convince Nancy that, whether or not she was reminded, paragraphs are an essential part of writing a paper. She had heard and focused on the information "a two-page paper," and that is where she stayed stuck. When your child exhibits this trait, it is exasperating for you and others who interact with him. It is also frustrating for your child because he is unable to see how he is interfering with his own success. In his discomfort, he often blames you and other authority figures for his problems. Power struggles between him and the one with whom he is interacting are a common result.

How the Child Copes with His Learning Disability

A child who is not learning is not a happy child. Outside of his home, school is where he spends the most of his waking hours. School is his job. When he cannot do his job successfully, he feels guilty. He feels bad about himself and his abilities. When a learning-disabled child is not identified early and given educational help and understanding, his frustration often results in behavior problems. He becomes either hostile and defensive toward the world or withdrawn from life. He lashes out, blaming others for his problems, or hides in shame, blaming himself for his inadequacies. How your child reacts to his learning problem seems to have more to do with his basic personality than with the severity of his disorder.

Neither the acting-out nor the withdrawn child is easy to live with. If your youngster is angry, blaming, and defensive, you can easily find yourself in power struggles with him. You are angry because he does not take responsibility for his actions. You feel hurt by the way he talks to you. An angry child can be mean and disrespectful. So can an angry parent. Although it is hard to admit, there are times when you want to do whatever is necessary to "make" him comply. You are tempted to try to get even for the way he has hurt you. Sometimes, instead of fighting it out, you give in to his demands. You are tired of fighting and giving in seems easier than using effective parenting strategies. Perhaps you do not even know an effective way to interact with your youngster when he is angry. Sometimes, within a single interaction, you respond first by fighting then with giving in. None of these ways of interacting with this unhappy child whom you love is satisfying to either of you.

The withdrawn, withering child, who is filled with shame and hopelessness, is not any easier to understand or live with than the hostile child. He hides in his shell, sharing neither his pain nor his joy with you. He acts helpless but rarely openly reaches out to you and others. He gains support by unconsciously manipulating the feelings of others. If you are the parent of a hopeless child, more than likely you feel as hopeless and helpless as he does. You try to rescue him from his pain. You control his environment, hoping he will experience success. When he does not respond, you feel either more hopeless or angry and ultimately withdraw from him. No matter what you do, your passive child does not seem to improve.

The LD child wants to succeed. He wants to learn, and he tries hard, at least in the beginning. When his academic attempts fail time after time, he resorts to inappropriate ways of gaining recognition. His desire to prove himself shows up in destructive ways. He is willing to get the attention he desires at almost any cost. He may become the tough kid on the block, the family rebel, or the class clown. He may become depressed, frightened, or needy. Although each of these roles brings him attention, none bring him the success he wants.

Social Patterns of Learning-disabled Children

Some children with learning disabilities escape the social and emotional distress commonly associated with the disorder. Many, however, suffer from unsatisfactory and unsatisfying peer relationships. When your child is not integrated into a supportive peer group, you ache for him because he has such a bleak social life. When you see him with his peers, it is clear that in some way he does not seem to fit in. Just as he has a lag in his academic skills, he also has a lag in his social development.

Most children develop social skills as a natural part of their maturation process. Through observation, modeling of what they see others doing, and the feedback they get from those in their environment, they become socialized. Many learning-disabled children do not learn effective social skills unless someone teaches them. They must be taught how to make friends, how to be a friend, and how to get along in groups, including their family. Skills of interacting successfully in the social world beyond family and friends must also be taught.

Some ineffective social traits commonly exhibited by LD children are over-sensitivity, insensitivity, temper tantrums, and immaturity. Perhaps your child is overly sensitive. He cries at the slightest provocation whether it is an "It's time to shape up" look from you or a playful insult from a peer. A cry-baby is an easy mark for less sensitive children.

The LD child can be insensitive to the feelings and needs of others. His insensitivity is expressed by acting like a bully, a tease, or a clown. His insensitivity can also be turned against himself. He does not recognize overtures of friendship from others and withdraws from social interaction by hanging on the fringe, having neither the courage nor the skills to enter into what is happening.

Your youngster may be well beyond the stage where temper tantrums are a relatively normal aspect of development, yet he tantrums regularly. The force of an older child's tantrums are frightening and angering to adults. Other children are confused by the behavior and perhaps even frightened by it. They label the tantruming youngster as being weird or a baby and do not like to play with him.

Many LD children choose friends who are younger than they are. This bothers parents. "Why won't he play with kids his own age?" they ask. Your child's social development probably lags behind that of his same-age peers. Since he lacks the skills his peers possess, associating with younger children is more comfortable and less threatening for him.

Diagnosis of the Learning-disabled

In the previous three sections of the chapter, we have described who the learning disabled are, how they cope with their disability, and common social patterns they exhibit. Looking at the child without knowing how he can be assisted to release his power for success is depressing. You know, though, that success is possible for these children in each facet of their lives. They are not hopelessly stuck in their disability. The steps to take to achieve that success are clear. The first is accurate diagnosis.

Learning disabilities are perplexing and frustrating. They result in academic underachievement and social and emotional pain if not diagnosed and properly treated early. Yet diagnosis is not easy. The disorder can mask as other problems, particularly in the young or mildly affected child. Nonetheless, a thorough and carefully administered evaluation will uncover a learning disability if it exists.

In diagnosing very young children who are considered at-risk for learning disabilities, the most crucial evidence seems to be related to their behavior as compared with expected developmental milestones. For example, does your three-year-old speak and use short sentences? Does your four-year-old speak in complex sentences using verb tenses, plurals, pronouns, and prepositions? Can your preschooler use his toys in a self-planned activity for an uninterrupted 10-minute period? Of course, each child develops at his own rate. It is the one who is chronically delayed that is of concern and needs to be monitored and possibly evaluated and remediated. Your child's preschool teacher and pediatrician can provide you with information on normal development. Ask for guidelines. If you are concerned about any aspect of your youngster's developmental progress, talk to his teacher or pediatrician. They want him to succeed as much as you do and are eager to be alerted to potential problems. There is nothing more heartening to a professional than catching a problem before it is fully developed.

Children of school age can be diagnosed more easily than preschool youngsters. The primary clue to watch for is poor academic success. Did your child have difficulty learning to read, write, or handle number concepts? Has he continued to lag behind? Does he seem bright in every way except school progress? Every child learns at his own rate; however, there is a range that is considered normal. If your child consistently falls out of this range, an evaluation is in order. Use the check list at the end of the chapter to determine if your youngster's underachievement is associated with signs of learning disability. If it is, discuss the problem with your pediatrician.

Remediation for the Learning-disabled

Although there is no cure for learning disabilities, the learning-disabled can be taught the skills they lack. The education process is twofold. First, the academic learning program emphasizes using the strengths the child possesses to remediate his weaknesses. The second, and equally vital part of his program, involves teaching him compensatory skills. These are the skills associated with functioning as an effective student in spite of his disability.

Having a learning disability does not mean your youngster must fail or have a minimal life. Many famous scientists, politicians, and people in the arts have been and are learning-disabled. Albert Einstein was not a typical learner. He had a poor memory, did not learn to read until he was nine, and could not solve math problems in the usual way. Thomas Edison had a reading and language disability, as did politician and philanthropist Nelson Rockefeller. Entertainers Tom Cruise and Cher have openly spoken about their learning disabilities. Pretty heady company for our learning-disabled children!

You and the professionals working with your youngster must be patient, understanding, and creative. Effectiveness with him necessitates giving up preconceived ideas of how children should learn. It demands an acceptance of the fact that your child needs to be taught what other children seem to pick up automatically.

Academic Remediation

Public schools offer several educational alternatives for learning-disabled students. The severity of the disorder determines which services are recommended. The most severely impaired children are educated in a special day class. All of the academic subjects are taught in this class. The youngsters are mainstreamed into regular physical education classes and some electives. Less impaired children receive services through a resource program. Students are pulled out of their regular classroom for remediation in their area of disability. They might receive resource programming in reading, language arts, math, or a combination of subjects. How much time a child can spend with the resource teacher is mandated by law and varies from state to state. Most LD students are educated through the resource room. Some districts are using an approach called the *consult model*. Under this program, the child stays in the regular classroom for all subjects and the resource teacher serves as a consultant to the classroom teacher to assist her with the learning-disabled students in her room.

Children with mild learning disabilities do not usually receive special services. The regular classroom program does not meet their needs, but they do not qualify for the resource program. Sensitive teachers attempt to individualize classwork for these youngsters so that success is assured. If your son or daughter has a mild learning disability, you may need to confer with the teacher each year to ensure that she is aware of the child's special needs.

The services of a private educational therapist are valuable regardless of the severity of the disability. Many needs of the LD child simply cannot be met through the school program as it exists in most districts. Budget demands are a prime determiner of how much a school district does for special-needs children. Rarely does a program provide for social, emotional, and academic needs to the degree necessary for optimal success. If your youngster does not receive any special academic assistance in school, private remediation is mandatory for success. An independent therapist usually recommends from one to three hours of therapy a week. Some therapists work in half-hour sessions, others prefer to keep the child for an hour. The youngster's age and attention span are guides in determining the length of each session. Fees for educational therapy vary widely and depend on factors such as the kinds of therapy employed and the person's credentials and training.

Whether your child is receiving academic help at school, privately, or both, the basic tenets for success are the same. The educational program must move slowly and sequentially and teach to the child's strong modalities while remediating the weak. This means that the educator begins teaching the child at his developmental level, regardless of his chronological age, and moves him toward a desired goal. She chooses methods which use his strongest learning modes and provides activities to strengthen his areas of weakness. Thus, visual, auditory, and kinesthetic abilities are used and strengthened. Each lesson must have a purpose related to an end goal and must provide numerous opportunities for success.

In addition to working with academic material, effective educational programming must teach compensatory skills. These skills are those which make the difference between a successful and unsuccessful student whether or not he is learning-disabled. They include such important issues as learning to write down assignments, taking notes, and structuring notebooks. Time management, study skills, organizational skills, and test-taking strategies are other compensatory skills. The best of students often need help in learning effective compensatory skills. The learning-disabled student must be taught the skills because they require the kinds of thinking that are often at the root of his disability.

Most learning-disabled children do not succeed when material is presented or required to be learned and completed in traditional ways. The willingness for parents and educators to break from old molds and ways of thinking is necessary if they are to assist these youngsters in releasing their power for success. Listening to prerecorded lectures or books, typing or taping homework assignments, and the use of calculators and computers are successfully used by some children. Any device which allows the child to express what he knows should be explored. There are no absolutes in how a child learns. Whatever way he best integrates material and can most clearly express what he knows is right for him. As educators and parents we must be open to unique avenues of teaching and self-expression.

Sometimes your child is making excellent academic progress, then hits a plateau or backslides. This is not unusual. Although it is frustrating to him, you, and his teacher, it is nothing to be alarmed about. It does not mean he has quit trying or learning. It may mean the particular method being used has quit working! This is where creativity is important in teaching the LD child. Just as we know that the learning-disabled child's progress and growth is inconsistent and erratic, we also know that sometimes what has been working excellently as a teaching tool becomes useless. We do not know why, only that it does. With patience, time, understanding, and creativity, another method will be found, and once again your youngster will be on an upward swing.

Social and Emotional Remediation in the School

Each of us needs love, nurturing, understanding, and positive experiences to grow into successful human beings. In parenting and providing professional care for the learning-disabled, assurance of successful growth takes careful planning. Love and nurturing are not enough. Positive experiences must be built into the child's life.

Your child's success in school requires a structured classroom. External structure provides safety and security for the LD child, since his own ability to organize his environment is not well developed. The ability to predict what is likely to happen in a given set of circumstances is one of the ways we feel successful and in control of our world. A structured classroom environment allows your child that ability. Structure in the physical room itself is necessary. He needs to know, for example, that homework is always put in the same basket on the same shelf each day. He needs to know that the materials he wants will always be found in the same place each time he seeks them. This ability to know his classroom structure without having to read signs or search for needed supplies provides the opportunity for probable success. When he is away from the classroom he can picture it in his mind and know what it looks like. Knowing provides security. Security leads to success.

Structure in the classroom schedule is important. Your youngster needs to know the sequence of events in the day. The LD child becomes confused by change. It does not challenge and motivate him. Change makes him feel anxious, unsure, and out of control. If he knows, for example, that reading is followed by math, as the reading period closes he begins to prepare himself mentally for math. He knows what to expect. He is predicting what will happen next, which allows him to feel in control of his life. Control leads to success.

Structure of classroom standards is vital. Knowing the rules and the consequences for not following them allows your child freedom of choice. He is in control of his destiny. Expectations must be stated in positive terms with the consequences for noncompliance clearly stated. Positive reinforcement for following classroom standards and follow-through for noncompliance assists the child in becoming aware of his behavior.

Sometimes when we discuss classroom structure with parents and teachers, the question of rigidity arises. "If we provide this kind of structure in the classroom, how will these youngsters adjust to the real world," is a typical question. We are not talking about structure without flexibility. We are talking about a framework. There are times when a classroom schedule must change. An assembly-day schedule is an example. In this or similar situations, it is important to prepare the child for the change. Each ordinary school day has a great deal of built-in flexibility. If the framework of structure that we have suggested is provided, the child accepts this flexibility and learns to adapt. In an unstructured or minimally structured environment, the learning-disabled child does not create his own structure and move ahead. He flounders, is anxious, and does not know what to do.

Part of the classroom program for the LD child needs to focus on his social skills. Whereas many children learn appropriate socialization simply by living in the family and interacting with children in the neighborhood and at school, the learning-disabled often need to be taught through planned activities. Games, stories, role-playing, and group discussions can benefit the child in this aspect of his growth.

Social and Emotional Remediation in the Home

Many of the same elements necessary for successful classroom experiences for the learning-disabled child are necessary for successful home life. Creating a home environment where successes are assured provides him with confidence in his worth as a human being. Children who feel good about themselves are happy. They contribute positively to the family. They carry their strong feelings about themselves into activities outside the home.

A regular routine in the home provides your child with the security of knowing what to expect. The routine includes getting-up and going-to-bed times as well as the activities throughout the day. Some families like to make a chart showing the routine so their child can refer to it if necessary. A charted day might look like this.

> **Monday**
> 7:00 get up and dress
> 7:20 sit down to breakfast
> 7:40 brush teeth; put lunch sack in book bag
> 7:50 leave for bus

SCHOOL

3:15 snack
3:30 begin homework or have quiet work time
4:30 play
6:00 dinner
7:00 TV
8:00 brush teeth, bathe, prepare for bed
8:20 choose and lay out clothes for next day
8:30 story or quiet game
8:45 bed

To some of you, this might seem too structured and rigid. Think a minute about your day. More than likely you do essentially the same activities at the same time each day. Structure is efficient. It ultimately allows for more freedom and flexibility than lack of structure does. Sticking to a general time frame and having the same sequence of events during the day is important in helping your youngster develop an internal structure. Most LD children are not well organized and need external guidelines to help them succeed. As your child incorporates effective living skills through appropriate school and home intervention, he begins to supply his own organizational abilities and fewer external controls are needed.

When the usual daily home routine needs to be changed, or extracurricular activities are added, forewarn your youngster so that he will not be upset or confused by the change.

Tom and his family had been in therapy for a year. When they first sought help, they all were highly frustrated because "nothing seemed to go right" in their home.

"We're a busy family," Tom's mother said. "Tom knows that, but he throws a fit almost every time we have an appointment or have to do errands. He's too young to stay home alone. He knows he has to go. Why does he make it so hard on us?"

Ten-year-old Tom was angry. He felt his life was out of his control. Choice was not something he experienced. He seldom knew what to expect when he got home from school. Could he play? Did his mom have plans for him? Did he have to go on errands? Moreover, he thought he was old enough to stay home alone in the afternoons. After all, his friends did!

Tom's parents learned to develop a family routine. The family sat together on Sunday evenings and discussed the activities that were planned for the week. The day before an out-of-the-ordinary event, Tom's parents reminded him it was coming. They reminded him again on the morning of the activity. For example, his mother might say, "Tom, remember that tomorrow is your dental appointment." Again on the day of the appointment she might say, "Tom, your dental appointment is at 4:00 this afternoon."

Tom's tantrums ceased, and he began taking part in some of the family decisions. He felt more at peace because he knew what to expect. As his parents recognized his greater cooperation, they began letting him spend short periods of time at home alone. Everyone in the family ended up a winner.

In every family, unplanned events occur. Whether it is an unplanned doctor's appointment due to illness or the fun of a spontaneous picnic, this kind of flexibility makes life interesting. It is not to be avoided. On a daily basis, most of a family's activities are known beforehand. It is the structure of the ordinary daily routine which helps your child function more smoothly and successfully.

As well as a routine in the home, a structured physical environment lends to your child's success. Two fundamentals in this environment are where he does his homework and where he puts his materials when he finishes his assignments. Your youngster needs a quiet place where he sits to do his homework each day. Whether it is at his desk in his room or at the kitchen table, it needs to be out of the family mainstream. It is essential to establish the homework place early in the school year so he associates it with homework. For the same reason, it is wise for him to do his homework at approximately the same time each day.

After his homework is completed, your youngster should put his books and assignments in a place where he can easily pick them up before leaving for school. Too often a child does his homework and forgets to take it to school or cannot remember where he put it after finishing it. If he always puts his materials in the same place immediately after finishing his work, he is more likely to successfully return them the following day.

Perhaps the most important way you can help your child in his social and emotional growth is through your communication with him. Be positive. Help him become aware of his successes by letting him know when he is doing well. Reinforce each little growth step he takes. Do not wait until a perfect goal is reached. Help him see the steps he is making toward the goal. Allow him to feel good about the process of reaching a goal. Appreciate him for his efforts.

Help your child succeed by following through when you make a request of him. For example, if you tell your daughter to go wash her hands and she does not, walk with her and stand beside her while she washes. When she finishes say, "Thank you for washing your hands." If you do not have time to follow through on what you ask, do not ask until you have the time.

Right now you are probably thinking, "I'm a busy parent. This will take far too much time. I cannot do all this." Effective parenting does take time. It is well worth the effort, however. If you are willing to work hard initially, the payoff comes later. Your child begins to develop his own controls, becomes more responsible for his behavior, and contributes to the family in a positive way. A capable child is a happy child. Your effective parenting allows your youngster to grow in his abilities and leads him toward his independence. A family that functions effectively provides a secure base for the child. When he feels secure, he is more successful both in and away from home.

What Can I Expect for the Future?

One of the first questions you may ask about your LD child is, "How long will it take for him to get better?" There is no single answer. Each child is different. Each family is different. A child who is severely disabled will probably not show improvement as rapidly as a less disabled child. The child who has experienced successes in some aspects of his life and who feels supported by his family will probably respond more quickly than the child who feels he does not fit anywhere. Instead of thinking about long-term predictions, it is more useful to take a present oriented view. What successes did I notice today, this week, this month?

Although daily growth in school may not be observable, certainly change should be apparent over a several week period. Keep in touch with your child's teachers on a periodic basis. Ask to see samples of his work if he does not bring work home regularly. Ask questions if you are concerned.

If your youngster is in private therapy, discuss the goals that have been set. Arrange an appointment for yourself every five or six weeks to evaluate his progress. Keep a list of questions you want to ask. Again, change will probably not be apparent on a daily basis. He should show signs of improved functioning by the third or fourth week of therapy. Progress in private therapy depends on the way in which each person involved in the process follows through on recommendations the therapist makes for work outside the therapy hour.

At home, be as consistent with your child as possible and watch for small changes in behavior. Reinforce the growth that you see. Remember that your learning-disabled child's growth and behavior change will probably be inconsistent. Slump times do not mean that he has reached his potential or that he is not trying. Keep your expectations reasonable, so that neither your nor your child will experience undue frustration. Do expect and look for success and growth, however.

Your child is first and foremost a child. He is far more like other children than he is different from them. With your love and the support of the school, the pediatrician, and the other professionals working with you as a team, your learning-disabled child can release his power for success and grow academically, socially, and emotionally.

Check List for Learning Disability

Following is a check list of characteristics commonly associated with learning disability. It does not include all possible symptoms. It does include the most frequently seen traits. If you find that your child exhibits 10 or more of the traits, discuss his behavior with your pediatrician.

	Yes	No
1. My child behaves inappropriately for his age.		
2. My child is frequently restless.		
3. My child is easily distracted.		
4. My child has a short attention span for his age.		
5. My child seems to "tune out" at times.		
6. My child appears lazy.		
7. My child does not adjust well to changes in routine.		
8. My child is uncooperative.		
9. My child frustrates easily.		
10. My child is difficult to discipline.		
11. My child does not perform consistently from day to day.		
12. My child frequently walks into things.		
13. My child frequently drops things.		
14. My child walks, runs, hops, skips, or jumps more awkwardly than his playmates.		
15. My child usually chooses to play with younger children.		
16. My child does not listen well.		
17. My child does not follow directions.		
18. My child has trouble remembering what he sees or hears.		
19. My child is usually forgetful.		
20. My child lags behind his age group in speech development.		

Continued . . .

	Yes	No
21. My child has difficulty naming familiar people and things.		
22. My child has difficulty expressing himself verbally.		
23. My child confuses right and left.		
24. My child has a tendency to work from right to left.		
25. My child writes poorly for his age.		
26. My child writes letters and numbers upside down or backwards.		
27. My child has difficulty understanding number concepts.		
28. My child reads poorly.		
29. My child has trouble sounding out words.		
30. My child sees letters or words in reverse.		
31. My child cannot understand what he reads.		
32. My child seems smart in everything except school.		

Check List for Evaluation of Services

The following check list will help you evaluate the services your child is receiving if he has already been diagnosed as having a learning disability. If he is not receiving the assistance he needs to release his power for success, speak to the classroom teacher or educational therapist. You may want to take this list with you.

	Yes	No
1. Following the diagnosis, my child's disability was explained to me in terms I understood.		
2. Options for intervention were presented to me.		
3. My child's disability was explained to him in terms he understood.		
4. If my child met the criteria for special programming through the public school, an IEP (Individual Educational Program) meeting was held.		
a. My child's case is reviewed annually at an IEP meeting.		
b. I am aware of the educational goals set for my child.		
c. My child is aware of the educational goals set for him.		
d. I am apprised periodically through conference or written communication about my child's progress.		
e. My child is apprised on a regular basis regarding his progress.		
5. If my child is receiving help from a private therapist, I am aware of the goals he is working toward. continued . . .		

	Yes	No
a. My child is aware of the goals he is working toward.		
b. I am apprised on a periodic basis in a face-to-face conference about my child's progress.		
c. My child is aware of the progress he is making.		
6. I have seen improvement in my child's social relationships.		
7. My child sees improvement in his social relationships.		
8. I can list at least three ways in which my child feels better about himself academically socially, and emotionally.		
9. My child can list at least three ways in which he feels better about himself academically, socially, and emotionally.		

9

The Child with
an Emotional Disorder

In today's fast-paced world, children experience a multitude of pressures. They are expected to do more faster and at an earlier age than ever before. Early entry into preschool allows toddlers to begin their education by age two. Kindergartners learn to read. Accelerated eighth-graders take high school courses. College-bound high school students enroll in advanced placement classes which give college as well as high school credit. Children learn sophisticated social behavior through the media. Ads interest the sandlot bunch in designer clothes. The message our youth receive is, "Grow up, push harder, NOW!"

Whether or not we agree that this fast pace is in our children's best interest, we get caught up in the momentum. Because we love our youngsters, we want to make sure that they receive the advantages society has to offer; educationally, that advantage currently focuses on acceleration. Children who either do not attend preschool or who attend for only one year prior to kindergarten may not be well prepared for the academically oriented programs provided in most kindergartens. When a child enters first grade, he is expected to know his numbers, letters, and the letter sounds. Those children who do not are behind before they ever begin their formal academic training. Middle school, junior high, and high school counselors encourage bright students to enroll in accelerated programs. The academic program of these students is so rigorous that elective courses are taken during a zero period either before or after the regular school day. After children and adolescents leave school for the day, they rush from one activity to another. They have sports, Scouts, clubs, church, piano and dancing lessons. A large group of adolescents have paid jobs.

As enriching as this life style may be, it comes with a cost. Unless parents recognize that they and their offspring do not have to get totally immersed in this whirlwind pace, the price that must be paid is in the form of physical, emotional, and educational problems. Many children and adolescents are chronically tired. A common response from adolescents to "How are you?" is "I'm really stressing!" Fatigue and stress cannot help resulting in less than optimal academic success. For many youngsters the result is underachievement.

Underachievement is nearly always accompanied by an emotional component. In some children, the emotional factor is a result of not succeeding academically. They feel anxious, depressed, or guilty about not doing well in school. This is called an emotional overlay. More often than might be expected, emotional problems are at the root of under-achievement. Only an adequate evaluation can distinguish between the two.

When a child is experiencing an emotional problem, parents blame themselves and each other more than in any other disorder leading to underachievement. They are often resistant to the diagnosis and perceive it as a personal threat to themselves and the existing family structure. Most parents have little accurate knowledge about emotional problems. What they know has come from novels and movies. Factual articles and television programs covering emotional problems often deal with severe forms of a disorder. Problems of a milder degree get little coverage.

The unknown frightens us. When your youngster is diagnosed with an emotional disorder, you may be afraid. Before your emotionally burdened child can receive the help that allows him to release his power for success, your fears must be assuaged. Knowledge and understanding allay fear. In the following pages you will learn about some emotional disorders that interfere with your youngster's ability to succeed in school.

What Is an Emotional Disorder?

There is no commonly agreed-upon definition for the term *emotional disorder*. Professionals in the various fields of mental health, as well as educators, each have their own specific criteria by which an emotional problem is defined and treated. Common elements exist across disciplines, however, which provide material for a general definition: an emotional disorder is characterized by behavior and/or perceptions which are inappropriate for the child's age and/or undesirable because it interferes with his own successful growth and development and/or the lives of others. This tells us that a child's behavior, how he perceives his environment, his age, his development, and how he affects the people in his life must be considered before a diagnosis is made.

Emotional problems range from those mildly affecting a child to those severely interfering with his ability to grow socially, emotionally, and academically. The moderately to severely disturbed youngster exhibits behavior which is concerning to parents and readily brought to the attention of the pediatrician or mental health worker. Symptoms of mild emotional problems are not as easily identified by parents and often go unrecognized until school achievement is affected, behavior problems develop, or physical complaints such as chronic stomachaches, headaches, or bedwetting require medical attention.

Emotionally disturbed children exhibit behaviors so varied and numerous they could fill a book. Their behavior differs from normal children's only in severity, duration of the behavior, and appropriateness of the behavior to a situation or the child's age.

> Julie was seven years old. Her parents said she had been difficult since birth. She had been colicky as a baby and cried several hours each day.
>
> During her toddler years, she was easily frustrated and expressed her discontent through tantrums. The tantrums increased in frequency and intensity as Julie grew older. Although she never had an outburst at school, she had them daily at home.
>
> One afternoon Julie's mother discovered large gouges on Julie's dresser top. Julie had attacked her dresser with a paring knife.

Julie's mother was frightened by this destructive behavior and sought professional help. The therapist diagnosed Julie's tantrums as the symptom of an unresolved emotional problem. Let's look at how Julie's diagnosis fits into our definition of an emotional disorder. First, her tantrums were an inappropriate way of expressing anger for her age. They had lasted well beyond the developmental stage where they are considered normal. Second, her daily outbursts interfered with her having successful relationships with her family. Finally, gouging the furniture impinged on the lives of other family members.

Just as a physician diagnoses and labels physical illnesses, mental health workers diagnose and name emotional disorders. Four of the most common resulting in underachievement are anxiety, oppositional behavior, adjustment problems, and concerns with identity during adolescence.

The Role of the Family with the Emotionally Disturbed Child

Each member in a family plays a role. Each has specific behaviors which are recognized and supported by other family members. As well as supporting positive, life-enhancing behaviors, it is not uncommon for individuals in the family to support unproductive behaviors in each other. For example, if Mary is seen as the "good" child and Megan as the "difficult" child, Mary believes it is to her benefit to support Megan's "bad" behavior. This allows her role of "good girl" to go unchallenged. This negative support can be in the form of tattling, teasing to elicit a "bad" response from Megan, or being especially cooperative and acceptable when Megan is having a difficult day. Support of unproductive behavior is not usually given consciously or "on purpose." Family members act without awareness on unrecognized beliefs.

When a child has an emotional disorder, his problem affects each member of the family to some degree. It affects how he is perceived in the family and how family members interact with him. The way in which his family relates to him can either assist him toward growth or unintentionally support his problem. The most effective therapeutic intervention involves the whole family at some point, so that each individual begins to see how his behavior affects others in the family. This does not mean that one family member has caused the emotional problem in another. It does mean that when each person in a family begins to respond with greater awareness, he can become a positive force in the well-being of every other person in the family.

The Overly Anxious Child

Take a minute and recall a time when you were worried or nervous. Remember how difficult it was to concentrate on what you were doing? You could not keep your mind on your activity because you were thinking about something that had happened in the past or was going to happen in the future. Maybe your neck or shoulders hurt because your muscles were tight. Perhaps you had a stomachache or headache. Probably you had trouble going to sleep at night. You were experiencing anxiety, and you did not feel good!

Usually your anxious, uptight feelings are associated with a specific situation like illness in a family member, financial problems, or an important decision you need to make. When the stressing event is over, your symptoms cease and you feel better. This kind of situational anxiety is not always the case. Some people feel nervous or scared most of the time. Their anxiety constantly interferes with their work and relationships.

Children feel anxious in the same ways you do. They cannot concentrate, they breathe shallowly or irregularly, experience physical disturbances, and have trouble sleeping at night. Many times they do not know what they are anxious about and do not know how to express what they are feeling.   Sometimes you can make a good guess at what is bothering your child. You know that moving to a new neighborhood, changing schools, the first day of school following summer vacation, and tests cause children and adolescents to respond with stress. Friendships, dating, and career choices create additional pressures for teens.

These situational stressors usually result in transitory or short-term anxiety. You can support your offspring by listening to his concerns and fears, accepting his feelings, and guiding him with love and understanding to help him through these uncomfortable times.

Understanding children is not easy. Sometimes your youngster is frightened or anxious and you have no idea what the cause is. You are not aware of anything is his life which is creating concern, and he cannot tell you what his problem is. Sometimes you are not even aware that your youngster is particularly upset until a poor progress report or parent conference indicates that he is not maintaining satisfactory achievement in school. On the other hand, you may be the parent of a child who is uptight all the time. You do not know why he cannot seem to relax. How do you know when the anxiety your child is experiencing is a problem which requires professional intervention?

The surest way of determining the extent of a problem is through an adequate evaluation, and there are signs to look for which can help you decide if an evaluation is warranted.

The first is the duration of the problem. If your son or daughter has been worried or anxious for three months or longer, an evaluation is in order. Something other than a situational stressor is probably at the root of his anxiety.

If your youngster is extremely self-conscious, needs constant reassurance in a variety of situations, is regularly concerned about his competence in academics and extracurricular pursuits, and is unrealistically concerned about past behavior or future events, professional intervention must be considered.

Finally, if physical complaints such as headaches, stomachaches, or the inability to relax have been determined to have no physical basis, your child may be experiencing an anxiety disorder which needs attention.

> Jonathan was seven. He was the oldest of three
> children. His parents were both well educated.
> He drove his parents crazy with his perfectionist
> tendencies. He insisted on getting to school early
> so he "wouldn't be late." He rarely finished his
> classwork or homework because each time he made
> an error, he started over so he "wouldn't have to erase."
> He was acutely aware of other peoples' behavior and
> readily pointed out what he perceived to be their
> shortcomings.

> Jonathan dressed meticulously and did not like to
> get dirty. He was not well liked by his peers. "The kids
> don't like me. They call me a nerd, but I don't care.
> They're all dumb," he said with a self-righteous air.

Jonathan's anxiety interfered with his success both academically and socially. His pain and feelings of isolation led him to adopt an attitude of superiority. Only through professional intervention did he learn how to become more comfortable and childlike.

Overly anxious children have a strong need to be right. They look to others for clues about what right is. Parents, teachers, and peers are the "experts" they rely on. They feel good about themselves when they meet the expectations of these experts. They are right, and right is good. When they do not meet the other's expectations, they feel wrong or bad. They do not trust their own judgment or consider it valid. They define their self-worth through the eyes of others. Because of their needs to be right and please others, some anxious children are high achievers. Many, however, underachieve. Their energy is tied up in trying to figure out what is right instead of in doing what needs to be done. Academically, this results in unfinished assignments and low test scores.

Intervention for the Overly Anxious Child

The goals of both therapy and effective parenting for the highly anxious child are the same: a greater reliance on inner direction for decision making, an increased variety of responses, and the ability to risk using those responses.

Since this child tends to see his behavior and that of others as either right or wrong, good or bad, he attributes extreme importance to his decisions and the response they receive. Professional intervention allows him to experiment with a wide range of behaviors. Within the limits of not hurting himself or another and of not being destructive, he is given the opportunity to express a variety of feelings and ideas. He and the therapist engage in both playing and talking. He is accepted for all his responses. He learns that it feels good to be flexible. He discovers that playing is fun. He sees that acting silly or using "bad" words does not result in dire consequences.

You may wonder if such intervention does not encourage inappropriate behavior outside the therapy room. Responsible therapy does not create children who misbehave. It helps a child recognize his own power of choice and how to use it wisely, become more inner-directed and less reliant on others for feelings of being okay, and to recognize that the consequences of wise choices are not life-threatening.

Educational remediation focuses on increasing academic skills. The child develops an effective set of work and study habits. He learns to work more quickly without sacrificing accuracy. He learns the process of arriving at answers. He discovers that in many subjects a correct answer can be stated in more than one way. He learns how to make a "good guess" when he is not sure of an answer and that giving a partial response is more effective than not responding at all. He learns to become a less rigid student.

Parenting the Overly Anxious Child

Effectively parenting the over-anxious child requires looking at your current parenting practices. Do you unwittingly encourage his dependence? Do you reinforce his actions which meet your expectations and ignore or punish those that do not? In many ways this child is easy to parent because he tries so hard to please that he rarely misbehaves. On the other hand, his tense, rigid approach to life can be frustrating.

You can help your child become more confident, relaxed, and playful. It demands your willingness to let him be more responsible for his own life. It means learning a different way of listening and responding. It means trusting that he is a capable human being.

When he asks you a question, and anxious children ask many, guide him to discover his own answer.

> Candi: Is this the right answer, Mom?
> Mom: Show me how you got your
>   answer, Candi.

> (Candi works a math problem)
> Candi: See, that's how I did it.
> Mom: Is your answer correct?
> Candi: Yes.
> Mom: Yes, it's exactly right. I'm glad you
>   figured that out by yourself.

Candi's mother gave her daughter the chance to validate herself instead of relying on an outside judgment of her correctness. She ended the interaction by encouraging Candi's behavior. This kind of response to the anxious child's search for validation is supportive and gives the message, "I know you are capable." It does not make the value judgment that Candi is "good" because she got the correct answer.

Give your child the opportunity to participate in the planning of his life.

> Mother: Brian, I'm going to the market.
>   Do you want to go or stay at home?
> Brian: Would I be alone?
> Mother: Yes. I'll be gone for about 15 minutes.
> Brian: And then you'll be right back?
> Mother: Yes. I will lock the door when I leave,
>   and you know not to answer it if
>   anyone comes. If the phone rings
>   you can leave it or answer it and say,
>   "My mother can't come to the phone
>   now. May I take a message?"
> Brian: I guess I'll stay.
> Mother: Okay. I know you'll do a
>   fine job while I'm gone.

Brian's mother gave him choice, information, and support. She did not try to convince him of his capability. She gave him the information he needed to make that decision for himself. She heard the concern behind his questions. Her responses reviewed "at home alone" behavior. She finished by supporting his capability.

Let your child know he does not have to be perfect.

Jeanine: Mom, I got a D on my math test.
Mother: Hmm. How do you feel about that?
Jeanine: Awful. I studied real hard. Honest.
Mother: I saw you studying last night.
Jeanine: I never did understand that stupid stuff.
Mother: It was difficult material.
Jeanine: You said it!
Mother: Another time could you do
        something differently?
Jeanine: I guess I should have
        asked for help.

Jeanine felt bad about her test grade. Her mother recognized that guiding Jeanine toward more effective behavior in the future was more important than discussing the grade itself. Her conversation with Jeanine let her daughter know she was an okay person even though she did poorly on the test. It also placed responsibility on Jeanine for seeking help when she needs it.

Anxious children do not need to be reprimanded and shown their inappropriate behavior. They are very conscious of it. They must be led to see their strengths and capabilities. The way you communicate with your child gives him the opportunity to recognize his worthiness.

The Oppositional Child

The oppositional child is aptly named. He opposes or is in conflict with anyone or anything that stands in his way. He is a defiant child and a rebel. Oppositional behavior is what parents refer to when they say about their toddler, "Oh, he's just in the terrible two's." During this stage of development the toddler's primary response is "NO!" He exerts his new-found independence through stubbornness, provocative behavior, and testing his parents' limits. Although annoying, if handled effectively, the behavior is short-lived and harmless.

Some children do not outgrow their defiance. Others may revert to it later in childhood or during adolescence. These children are argumentative, lose their tempers easily, are stubborn and resentful. They defy rules and blame others when they experience difficulty. They engage in power struggles with parents and other authority figures. Peer and sibling relationships suffer.

> Nine-year-old Steven sat in the office glaring at his mother. "I told you I can't do my homework because I have too many chores," he said through clenched teeth. He held onto the chair so tightly his knuckles were white.
>
> "But you don't do your chores," replied his mother struggling to maintain her control.
>
> "How do you know? You're never home when I get home from school," yelled Steven.
>
> "I know because I can see they haven't been done, and you're always watching TV." Steven's mother stared at him angrily.
>
> "How am I supposed to do all this stuff when nobody's there to remind me?" chided Steven.

Steven and his mother were in a no-win argument. Both needed to be right. Arguments like this are familiar to you if you live with an oppositional child. Both you and he are so eager to prove a point, neither of you hears the feelings the other is expressing.

If your child exhibits oppositional behavior, you probably think he is bad or naughty. Often you are sure he cannot do anything right. You are angry at him more than loving. You feel guilty because you find yourself disliking him. When you do express love or affection, he does something to annoy you or push you emotionally away. Although his behavior is most common at home, it may carry over to school and sometimes into extracurricular activities.

It is difficult to accept, but this is your youngster's way of letting you know he needs help. He is hurting and does not believe that anyone, especially you, understands him. His exasperating behavior is an ineffective way of saying, "I need you to do something. I don't know what, but my life isn't working. Help me."

The oppositional child is always an underachiever. Not doing well in school is a sure way of "getting" most parents, and this child is a pro at pushing parents' buttons.

Intervention for the Oppositional Child

Early therapeutic intervention is imperative if positive results are to be realized with these children. The probability for success lessens as they grow older. Some turn their defiance into greater deviant behavior in later adolescence and adulthood. Others, though they may become professionally successful, continue to be difficult to get along with and seem to fight life every step of the way. They are not happy people. If your child has exhibited oppositional behavior for six months or longer, intervention is warranted.

An effective therapist-child match is particularly important when working with this disorder. The child must be able to develop a trusting relationship with the therapist so he can learn to participate nondefensively and noncombatively in the counseling process. If he perceives that the therapist is judging, critical, or controlling, he will be unable to let go of his own controlling behavior and explore more effective ways of interacting.

Although the oppositional child is not aware of it, his behavior is far more detrimental to him than to those he is trying to hurt or punish. Counseling helps him recognize the role he plays in creating the negative consequences he experiences. New, more effective responses are learned and practiced.

Anger, hurt, and feelings of unworthiness are at the root of defiant behavior. Through both play therapy and talking, the child becomes aware that these are the feelings he wants someone to understand. The therapist helps him learn to let others know in appropriate ways what he is feeling so that he does not have to act out with destructive behavior.

When academic remediation is required, and it usually is, attention is given to increasing academic skills and developing compensatory skills.

The acting-out child often uses school work as a weapon of control. He fails to do his homework, complete his classwork, or prepare for tests. The tutor or educational therapist teaches him how to organize his time and materials. She shows him how to set priorities for his tasks. She helps him learn how to study and prepare for tests and instructs him in effective test-taking techniques.

Parenting the Oppositional Child

Effectively parenting this child is a challenge. He knows how to push your buttons so that you respond in an authoritarian, controlling way. You probably feel frustrated at your inability to form a satisfying relationship with him and frightened because you feel out of control when you are interacting with him.

Parents of defiant children commonly complain that they have tried everything and nothing works. To them it seems that way. Probably they have simply done whatever they had done before in a slightly different way or by using different words. Most parents know how to parent in only one way. They believe they must be in control and be right. They unconsciously set up an "I am superior, you are inferior" relationship with their children. If this sounds like your family, you know this creates fuel for your oppositional child's fire. He does not respond to traditional forms of discipline. He simply rebels harder.

> Dad: I told you to take out the trash.
> Mike: I said I'd do it when this show is over.
> Dad: I said NOW! (Dad walks over and turns off the TV.)
> Mike: Okay, okay. I'll dump your stupid trash.
> Mike dumped the trash, but only half of it went into the barrel. The rest fell on the ground and blew down the alley.

Mike's method of emptying the trash said, "You might think you can make me do this, but you can't make me do it right." Parenting an oppositional child works best when he is encouraged to use his power constructively. This is done by enlisting his cooperation in as many aspects of family life as you can come up with creatively. For example, Mike's dad might have handled the trash situation this way.

> Dad: I'd like you to take out the trash when
> your show is over.
> Mike: But my very favorite show comes on next.
> I can't do it till after that.
> Dad: I'll tell you what. It's 5:00 o'clock now.
> We'll be eating dinner at 6:30. It'll be fine
> with me if you make sure the trash is
> emptied by dinner.

Mike now had the opportunity to choose when he wanted to do his chore, yet he still had a time frame to work into. His dad did not fall into the trap of arguing about Mike's excuse that he had another show he wanted to watch. He simply set reasonable perimeters for the job.

Family rules can be determined in a meeting with each family member participating. Consequences for noncompliance can be negotiated together.

> Mom: I think curfew should be set at midnight.
> Melissa: That's not fair. What if a dance isn't
> over till 11:30?
> Mom: What do you think is a reasonable curfew?
> Melissa: I don't think there should be a set one.
> Dad: We need to set some limits on how late
> you'll be out.
> Melissa: What about two hours after a dance or show
> ends?
> Mom: I think that's too much time.
> Dad: How does one hour sound, Melissa?

> Melissa: I guess it's okay, but sometimes it
> might have to be later.
> Dad: For special occasions we can negotiate.

Melissa is more likely to respect the curfew since she had some input into the decision. In her family, the consequence for not making curfew was to forfeit her hour after the next event she attended. She determined the consequence herself. When you encourage a child to participate in decisions that affect him and allow him to experience the positive or negative consequences that result, he is learning responsible behavior.

Too often, parents forget to notice when their offspring follow the rules.

> Cathy sat with her mother discussing how some
> of the changes they had implemented in their family
> were working.
> "I like everything but one thing," said Cathy.
> "What's that?" asked her mother.
> "Well, you always tell me when I'm wrong,
> but you don't say anything when I do things
> right."

Children are attuned to your attitudes. They want your attention and approval. If they believe their cooperative behavior is not noticed, it is not worth their effort to work within the family guidelines. They would rather risk doing what they want to do and getting your negative attention. "But they ought to behave," you say. Perhaps so, but people usually do the thing that brings them the attention they desire. To increase the likelihood of cooperative behavior, recognize it and encourage it. Catch your child "being good."

Another trap parents of defiant children fall into is not letting them experience the consequences of their behavior.

> Jim often forgot to take his lunch to school.
> Several times a week, his mother delivered it to
> the school for him.

>During a counseling session, the therapist
>and Jim's mother were discussing whether or
>not this encouraged him to become more re-
>sponsible about remembering his lunch. His
>mother said, "But sometimes I feel so sorry
>for him. So little goes right for him. I at
>least want him to have his lunch."

You feel a tremendous amount of anger at your defiant child. Like Jim's mother, you also feel sorry for him. You do not want him to experience more hurt and humiliation than he already does. Rescuing him from irresponsible behavior is not how to help him. The rescuing only reinforces your position of power. It does not contribute to the growth of responsible cooperation in him. Instead, express confidence in his abilities; over time, it pays big dividends. Defiant children are used to being recognized for their faults. Minimize the attention you give to your youngster's uncooperative behavior and express your confidence and appreciation in his ability to succeed. Your confidence in him increases his confidence in himself. For all his bravado, he feels unsure inside. He needs and wants your support.

The Child with Adjustment Problems

Aware parents know that new or unusual events create stress for their children. They are not surprised when the birth of a sibling, a change of schools, or the death of a grandparent results in a period of discomfort or adjustment. Children react to stress by acting out or withdrawing, by feeling anxious or depressed. You recognize these symptoms because you know that you, too, feel out of control, anxious, or depressed when confronted with similar issues.

Sometimes children are unable to adjust or grow through stressing situations. Their symptoms last well beyond what is considered a reasonable adjustment period, or they have an overly strong reaction to the event. If the stressor is ongoing, such as prolonged illness in a family member or a parent who has lost a job and not found another, a child may be unable to achieve a level of adaptation which allows him to function successfully. When these reactions occur, it is labeled an adjustment disorder.

> Erin's family moved to a new city during the summer between her fifth and sixth grades. Although there were children in her new neighborhood, she refused to play with them. She spent most of her summer reading and writing letters to her friends in her old community.
>
> When school began in the fall, she did not know anyone. She made no effort to make friends with the girls in her class. Initially the girls tried to befriend her. When she did not respond, they thought she was stuck up and ignored her. Her old friends wrote to her less frequently as they got reinvolved in their own school activities. Erin felt isolated and alone. She withdrew into herself and began spending most of her time in her bedroom with the door closed.

Erin was depressed. She was unable to accept her family's move and involve herself in her new school and peer group. She was experiencing an adjustment problem. Adjustment disorders are accompanied by anxiety, depression, or a combination of anxiety, depression, and other emotions. The anxious child manifests the symptoms that we talked about in our discussion of the over-anxious youngster. The primary symptoms are nervousness and worry. Depressed children are withdrawn. Often they are tearful for no apparent reason, and they live with a sense of hopelessness. They may complain of constant fatigue or have insomnia. Feelings of inadequacy and a lack of enthusiasm for previously enjoyed activities are common. The youngster may be unable to attend to task. The child with mixed emotional features exhibits a combination of emotions. An example is the adolescent who enters his freshman year in high school. He reacts with anxiety prior to the beginning of school, is depressed when he discovers that none of his friends are in any of his classes, responds with anger at the amount of homework that is expected of him, and vacillates between arrogant independence and childlike dependence during his adjustment period. Underachievement is common when children are experiencing adjustment disorders.

With appropriate intervention, adjustment problems are relatively short-lived. The symptoms disappear or a new level of adaptation is reached. As the child begins to adapt to his new life situation, his behavior and academic difficulties return to their pre-stressor level.

Intervention for the Child with Adjustment Problems

Counseling is the recommended treatment for children with adjustment problems. It is valuable for youngsters to work out their feelings with someone who is neutral in their situation. The counselor assists the child to see his problem clearly. She provides a safe environment for him to explore his feelings through talking and playing. Behavior options are discovered. Role-playing with the therapist gives the child an opportunity to practice new ways of behaving and interacting with others. Counseling provides the extra support a child needs in learning to adapt to new or unexpected events in his life. This support is particularly valuable if you, too, are feeling stressed. When the adults in a child's life are in turmoil, he feels even more helpless or anxious. When you take part in the counseling, the counselor can help you better understand your child's reactions and assist you in guiding him through his adjustment period. She can be a sounding board for your frustrations and anxieties.

Although academic problems are usually transitory in children with adjustment problems, tutoring can be useful during the adjustment period. Declining grades, the inability to concentrate, and difficulty with memory which can occur during stressful times add to the pressures the child is experiencing. The assistance of a tutor allows him to stabilize his academic work as he adjusts to his otherwise changing world.

Parenting the Child with Adjustment Problems

What your child needs most during this time of adjustment to new or uncomfortable conditions in his life is your love, understanding, and support. If prior to his problem you and he had a caring relationship based on trust and with effective communication, his symptoms will be easier for you to accept than if your relationship was not satisfactory. If the event causing discomfort is also stressful for you, empathy and understanding will be harder. It is difficult to nurture and support when you, too, are feeling needy.

When your child is hurting, it is easy to get caught up in his pain. It is necessary to be caring and to empathize with his hurt without being a part of it. If you express as much upset by his pain as he does, he feels hopeless and frightened. It is effective to listen and reflect to him the feelings that you hear.

> Cameron: Everybody hates me.
> Mother: You feel very left out.
> Cameron: I don't even want to go to school tomorrow.
> Mother: It's scary to go when you're afraid
>   nobody will pay attention to you.
> Cameron: Oh, well, maybe it'll be
>   better tomorrow.

Through careful listening, Cameron's mother was supporting her daughter. She did not give her solutions to her problem nor did she try to "make it better" for her. When we solve others' problems for them, we rob them of the opportunity to discover that they are capable of generating their own answers and inner support. Solving problems for others is an authoritarian stance. It keeps the other dependent on us. Usually when we attempt to solve our children's problems for them, our suggestions are met with a negative response. Our solution is not quite good enough; not quite the response they were looking for. If we are attached to having their answer for them, their negative response can seem ungrateful. The stage is set for a power struggle. "But shouldn't Cameron's mother try to help her know what to do?" you are asking. Not unless Cameron asks for or indicates she would like help. Just knowing you understand her dilemma is often enough for your youngster.

Instead of solving his problems for him, encouraging your child toward healthy behavior without insisting that he change gives him options he may not see.

> Todd's girlfriend told him she didn't want to "be so serious." She wanted to start dating other boys. He felt hurt and rejected. He locked himself in his room, closed the blinds, and put on his headphones and music. He did not join the family for dinner.
>
> He remained in his room all the following day, except for making a sandwich which he took to his room to eat.
>
> Late in the afternoon, his dad knocked on his door. Todd allowed him to enter. His dad expressed his sadness for Todd's situation and invited him to go for a run. Todd declined. His father then indicated he'd be available for dinner or a show later that evening. Todd elected to go to the show.

Todd's father did not try to take away his son's pain. He did not insist that Todd begin interacting with the family. He offered Todd opportunities. Todd chose an activity where he could be with his dad yet not have to interact with him. It was a safe way to begin moving out of his isolation.

Respecting your child's feelings, supporting and encouraging him, and getting professional guidance when necessary will assist him in moving through an adjustment problem.

The Adolescent with an Identity Disorder

Adolescence is the transition between childhood and adulthood. From the time a young person is 12 or 13 until he is 19 or 20, he struggles with discovering who he is and how he fits into the world. Most youth have periods of turmoil during this search. Some experience more severe stress: stress which affects their relationships and academic functioning. Mental health professionals label this greater-than-normal stress an identity disorder. These disturbed adolescents have a weak sense of self. They exhibit intense distress about the uncertainty surrounding the basic issues which relate to identity. They wrestle with the same questions as those absorbing all adolescents—questions about schooling and career, religion and the meaning of life, friendship patterns and sexual behavior, long-term goals and moral values—but they are unable to accept their confusion as temporary. They do not reach a level of adaptation which allows them to lead effective lives. As well as underachieving and having relationship problems, these youth rebel more intensely than their peers who are not chronically disturbed. They are at high risk for substance abuse and at higher risk for suicide than their peers.

In families where there is trust and a sense of caring and respect, youth can feel safe about exploring the issues involved with growing toward adulthood. They have a strong base and know they are supported as they journey into the world to discover who they are. When there is lack of communication and trust in their family relationships, they must struggle on their own.

Sam was 17 and a senior in high school. Although he had never participated in school activities, he had been a B and C student until his junior year. During the spring semester of his junior year, he started cutting classes. In the fall semester of his senior year he ditched one or two days a week. He spent the days with his girlfriend whom he had met at the pizza restaurant where he worked over the summer. Several months into their relationship she was pregnant.

Sam's parents were successful professional people. They had effective relationships with their two younger sons. Their relationship with Sam had been stressful since his childhood. When he entered high school, it disintegrated further. With Sam's

current problems, they were ready to "throw him
out of the house."

    "We've never been able to trust him," said Sam's
father. "This just proves we were right about him."

    "They never let up," said Sam. "They snoop in
my stuff and always act like I'm on drugs or something.
They always call to see if I'm where I'm supposed to be.
I just gotta get away and find out what's happening."

Sam was confused and afraid. He had not experienced the support of
his family as he grew up, and he certainly did not have it now. In his search
for discovering more about himself and for independence, he made some
decisions that were not in his best interest. Instead of guiding him toward
more appropriate choices, his parents focused on his inabilities and their
lack of trust in him. His attempts at accomplishment, like his job at the
pizza restaurant, were not acknowledged as successes. They were recognized as "what he should have been doing all along." Sam was a young man
who was hurting and badly in need of guidance.

Intervention for the Adolescent with an Identity Disorder

If your teenager has been exhibiting symptoms of distress for three
months or longer, he is crying for help. Counseling for distressed adolescents is imperative. They need an adult they trust with whom they can
discuss their problems and to whom they can turn for guidance and support.
The sensitivity and objectivity of a counselor guides a teenager toward
greater understanding of himself and his environment. Through values
clarification she can assist him in discovering what he believes in, what he
wants, and how to positively assert his independence. When the family
participates in the counseling process, the possibility is open for new
patterns of interaction among family members to emerge.

Most adolescents struggling with identity issues underachieve academically. Their energy is depleted in trying to cope with their feelings and
their struggle for successful independence. Educational remediation can

be useful in assisting them through this difficult time; however, often they are not interested in academic help. For some, not performing in school is part of their rebellion. When this is the case, remediation goes against the statement they are attempting to make. If your teen asks for educational help or shows an interest in improving his skills or grades, by all means provide the opportunity. Do not try to push assistance on him. Your insistence will be interpreted as intrusion in his life and will not aide in creating the climate for an effective relationship with him. Remediation can only work if he is open to it. When he is ready, he himself will initiate the needed steps for academic improvement.

Parenting the Troubled Teen

When your teenager is in crisis, you experience a range of conflicting feelings. You are afraid, sad, and angry. You feel helpless and rejected. You are not sure how to reach out to him, and when you try, your attempts are not accepted in the way you would like them to be.

Regardless of how poor your relationship with your youngster is, he wishes it were better just as much as you do. He is afraid of being hurt by you as much as you fear his rejection. Both of you are unhappy. Since you are the adult, initially the steps toward more effective relating fall on your shoulders. You probably do not think this is fair. You would like your youngster to take equal responsibility. He cannot. It is up to you to keep the door for relating open. In some cases it means reopening a door that has been closed. There are ways you can do this, and when they are used consistently, positive change occurs. Patience is required. Your relationship with him did not disintegrate overnight. It cannot improve that quickly, either. If you honestly attempt to relate effectively with your youngster, he will, in time, respond.

In as many ways as you can, show your teen that you recognize his successful behavior. The successes are not always easy to find, but look. They are there.

Bob's curfew was midnight. At 12:20 he came in, locked the door, turned on the alarm, and turned

out the lights. His father stepped into the hall as he
passed his parents' bedroom door. "I know I'm late,
but I couldn't help it," said Bob. "I had to take
everybody else home."

"I'm glad you're home safely. Thanks for locking
up and setting the alarm," said his dad.

Bob's parents were in counseling to learn to effectively relate to their
son. "For right now, recognize the positive behavior and ignore the other
as much as possible," their counselor suggested. That is what Bob's father
did. Bob did not need to be told he was late. He already knew that. When
his dad acknowledged his positive actions even though he was late, he felt
appreciated. Since his dad did not challenge his explanation for being late,
he felt trusted. The way Bob's dad handled the situation left the door open
for communicating and relating.

In addition to recognizing successful behavior, show your adolescent
that you trust him and the choices he makes.

Stefanie's grades had been poor during her
sophomore year. She was currently working on a
study contract set up with her school counselor and
teachers. At the third grading period her grades
showed minimal improvement.

When her parents received the grade card they
sat down with Stefanie. "We know you've been
completing your homework and studying more
regularly for tests," said her mother. "We appreciate
your effort."

Although her report card did not strongly reflect her increased effort,
the way Stefanie's parents chose to communicate with her indicated that
they were aware of her changed behavior. By paying attention to her
positive behavior instead of her grades, they were saying, "We know you
are carrying out your commitment to your contract."

Teenagers have difficulty recognizing small growth steps. They need
to be acknowledged regularly so that they do not become discouraged. It

is nearly impossible to be too supportive, so be liberal with your encouragement.

> Molly and her 15-year-old daughter Angela were
> in counseling together. Molly thought Angela was too
> dependent, and Angela didn't think her mom paid
> enough positive attention to her.
>
> "If Angela asks me once whether I think she's done
> a good job on something, she must ask me 50 times,"
> said Molly. "I get sick of her wanting so much
> attention. "Isn't it enough when I say once that she's
> done well?"
>
> "But Mom, you never notice when I do anything right.
> All you talk to me about is what I don't do," said Angela
> tearfully. "Even when I do something to surprise you,
> you don't even pay attention."

Angela was a girl who needed more support than many 15-year-olds. Molly was a woman who found it difficult to be supportive in the best of times. The extra amount of support that Angela needed was annoying to her. When youngsters can count on receiving regular, sincere recognition from their parents, they usually become less needy. Initially, Molly had to force herself to look for actions to support and encourage in Angela. In a very short time, Angela stopped demanding that her mom recognize her, and Molly began to notice that Angela was more successful than she previously had given her credit for being.

Your teenager wants and needs your love and support. He needs space provided with guidance. He needs to feel independent. He needs to feel that you trust him and are there as a base for him. The greater his struggles, the more he needs to know from you that he is okay. His rebelliousness and other distressed responses to his adolescence are signals that he is hurting and needs help.

Your youngster's adolescent years are not any easier for you than they are for him. You are grappling with all of the issues involved with effectively parenting an older child. His growing independence from you creates a time of change and transition in your life that you need to work through. His difficult times are hard for you and on you, and you may not feel you have the resources to handle them. You do not have to weather them alone. If you need to, get some professional help and support for yourself. Read books that focus on parenting teens. Take a parenting class. Take care of yourself and your needs so you can be effectively and lovingly there for him.

In Conclusion

Emotional problems are a common cause of underachievement. A problem may be mild and short-lived, or it may be more severe and take longer to correct. Regardless of the intensity, early recognition and intervention is necessary. Underachievement and poor social and family relationships need not cripple your child. Psychological counseling, parent counseling or education, and academic remediation can assist him in releasing his power for scholastic, social, and emotional success.

Check List for Emotional Disorders

The following is a check list of characteristics commonly associated with emotional disorders leading to underachievement. It does not include all possible symptoms. It does include those seen most frequently. If you find that your youngster exhibits at least six of these traits, he may be experiencing emotional distress. Pay attention for further signs and seek professional help if necessary. If he has exhibited 10 or more traits for a period of three months or more, he is showing symptoms of an emotional disorder which warrants professional intervention. If your teenager abuses alcohol or uses drugs, he needs immediate professional assistance for handling these problems.

	Yes	No
1. My child has many headaches.		
2. My child has many stomachaches.		
3. My child has trouble going to sleep at night.		
4. My child always seems tired.		
5. My child cries easily.		
6. My child worries about his health.		
7. My child worries about the health of other family members.		
8. My child worries about doing the right thing.		
9. My child worries about school.		
10. My child worries about his future.		
11. My child is self-conscious.		
12. My child needs lots of reassurance.		
13. My child always seems uptight.		
14. My child has difficulty following rules at home.		
15. My child has difficulty following rules at school.		
16. My child has temper tantrums.		
17. My child cannot take "no" for an answer. continued . . .		

	Yes	No
18. My child constantly argues with me.		
19. My child argues with other adults.		
20. My child is stubborn.		
21. My child constantly tries to provoke me.		
22. My child overreacts to situations.		
23. My child is depressed.		
24. My child isolates himself from others.		
25. My child's grades have dropped.		
26. My child is unable to concentrate.		
27. My teenager's interest in school has declined.		
28. My teenager and I are unable to communicate positively about any subject.		
29. My teenager is confused most of the time.		
30. My teenager does not make decisions that contribute to his welfare.		
31. My teenager abuses alcohol.		
32. My teenager uses drugs.		

Check List for Evaluation of Services

The following check list will help you evaluate the services your child is receiving if he has already been diagnosed as having an emotional disorder. If he is not receiving the assistance he needs to release his power for success, speak to the professional working with your family. You may want to take this check list with you.

	Yes	No
1. After the diagnosis, my child's problem was explained to me in terms I understood.		
2. Recommendations for treatment were discussed.		
3. My child's problem was explained to him in terms he understood.		
4. My child does not resist going to therapy.		
5. I participate in some of the therapy sessions.		
6. I have a session on a planned basis to increase my repertoire of parenting skills.		
7. My child's symptoms are not as intense as they were prior to the initiation of therapy.		
8. I can verbalize at least three ways in which my child is feeling better about himself academically, socially, and emotionally.		
9. My child can verbalize at least three positive statements about himself academically, socially, and emotionally.		

10

The Child Who Is a Slow Learner

Human beings spend a large part of their time watching other human beings. People-watching is entertaining, educational, and enlightening. It is enjoyable to pass the time in a check-out line at the supermarket watching other shoppers or to watch other spectators at a sporting event during a lull in the game. It is a valuable learning experience to watch someone who is skilled at a task we want to master. It is enlightening for us as parents to have the opportunity to observe our youngster when he does not know he is being watched. When we people-watch, we make assumptions about what we see, and we label it. Our assumptions are based on what we believe is happening, and the labels we choose are our judgments about the situation. For example, if we see someone crying, we might assume the person is sad and label the situation as being "a shame" or "too bad." Sometimes our assumptions and labels are correct. Just as often, they are not. When we people-watch for entertainment, it makes little difference what we assume about our observations and how we label them. When we are observing others as an educational experience, assumptions and labels can inhibit our own progress but are harmless to those we are watching. If we are watching another to gain enlightenment about that person, our assumptions must be carefully validated and our labels cautiously chosen.

There is a group of children who do not excel in school and who look like underachievers. They do not learn as quickly as their classmates and do not perform most academic tasks at grade level. It can easily be assumed that these youngsters are underachieving, and they may be labeled under-achievers.

They are not. They are children who are slow learners. The slow-learning child is easily confused with the underachiever because he exhibits similar traits. He does not finish his classwork in the expected amount of time. The quality of his work is not up to grade-level expectation. He may try to avoid classwork and homework. His social and emotional life may be impaired. It is only through an evaluation that slow learning is distinguished from underachievement. Early diagnosis of the condition leads to intervention which alleviates unneeded frustration and pain for the child and gives him the opportunity to release his power for success.

When an evaluation of your youngster reveals the diagnosis of slow learner, your heart may sink. This diagnosis leads to sadness in many parents. You love your child, and the knowledge that he is not intellectually bright is concerning and disappointing. You want him to be successful in school and later in a career. You have hopes and dreams for him that you are afraid will not be realized if he does not learn easily. You have questions. What exactly is a slow learner? Does it mean he is retarded? How well will he be able to learn? Can my youngster go to college? What about jobs? As you might imagine, some of these questions have straight-forward answers. Others cannot be answered as easily.

Before we move into discoveries about the slow-learning child, we want to answer another question. If a slow learner is not really an underachiever, why is he a part of this book? There are two reasons. The first we have alluded to already. The slow learner disguises as an underachiever. Secondly, a slow learner can also be an underachiever. He may not be attaining the academic level he is capable of achieving. In either case, the reason this child is not working at grade level must be determined. If he is a slow learner working to capacity, his educational program can be modified to meet his needs. If he is both a slow learner and an under-achiever, appropriate steps can assist him toward greater success.

Who Is the Slow Learner?

Although everyone knows there are differences in intelligence among people, most do not know that there is a pattern to the distribution of intelligence throughout the population. When this pattern is plotted onto a graph, it forms what is called a bell-shaped curve. It is called this because it has the symmetrical shape of a bell.

The middle and largest section of the curve represents approximately half or 50% of the population. This group have what is referred to as average or normal intelligence. As the curve begins to flatten out to the right, two smaller groups equaling 22 or 23% of all people are represented. These groups are intellectually high average and superior. As the curve flattens to the left, another 22 or 23% of the population is represented by two categories called low average and borderline. Finally, at each extreme end of the curve, two very small segments of the population are represented. Each group contains just more than 2% of all individuals. At the upper or right end of the curve are those with very superior intelligence. At the lower end are those who are mentally deficient or mentally retarded.

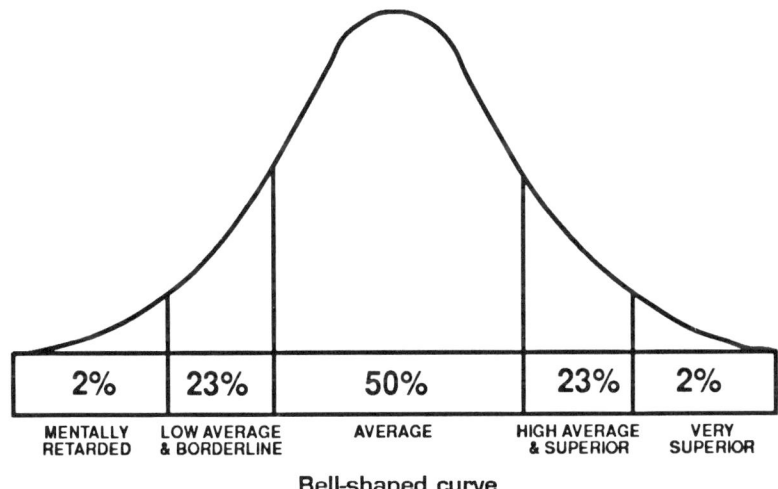

2%	23%	50%	23%	2%
MENTALLY RETARDED	LOW AVERAGE & BORDERLINE	AVERAGE	HIGH AVERAGE & SUPERIOR	VERY SUPERIOR

Bell-shaped curve

When the term *slow learner* is used, it refers to that 22 or 23% of the people who fall into the low average or borderline categories. Generally, the IQ or number score received on an intelligence test by the slow learner falls somewhere between 75 and 90.

You remember from the discussion of intellectual functioning in chapter 4 that the IQ score itself is relatively unimportant. It does not show where a person's learning strengths are, nor does it indicate how well an individual uses his abilities. To understand the plight of the slow learner, however, talking about number scores in general serves a valuable function.

In most schools, classrooms are set up according to children's chronological age. For example, in a first-grade class, the majority of children are six years old for much of the school year. In a fifth-grade class, most of the students are 10 years old. Classroom curriculums, or courses of study, are created to meet the needs of the greatest number of students in a given grade. Since about half of all people fall into the average range of mental ability, you can guess that in most classrooms about half the children will have average intelligence. It is with this group of children in mind that textbooks are written and curriculums planned. What about the abilities of the other half of the class?

> Ms. Romano's fifth-grade class had 31 students.
> On a group intelligence scale administered to the
> children, the results were as follows: 17 children
> scored in the average area of intellectual functioning;
> five children achieved high average, and one made
> superior scores; eight students fell within the low average
> range and none in the retarded area of mental ability.
> On an academic achievement test, the scores
> ranged from second-semester second grade to first-
> semester ninth grade.

Ms. Romano's class was not unusual. Most classrooms have students with a wide range of abilities. In fact, it can be expected that most public school classrooms serve children who function academically from approximately two years below to two or more years above grade level. If one were to look at number scores, theoretically, the IQ range in a regular classroom could be from 75 to 130!

As you can see, the slow learner is at an extreme disadvantage. He simply does not possess the intellectual skills to successfully compete in the academic marketplace. Neither does he qualify for any academic assistance through the public school system. He is the child who is least served by our schools as they currently exist. Teachers and parents of slow-learning children must recognize their predicament and provide the necessary academic and emotional support for them, so that they can release their power for success and grow into secure, well-functioning individuals.

Tracy was a fifth grader. Learning had not come easily to her from the time she had been in first grade. She was placed in the lowest reading and math groups and managed well until fourth grade. In her fourth grade year, she could not keep up with her classmates at all. She was a hard-working child and participated cooperatively in the classroom. Although she was not well-liked by her classmates, neither was she strongly disliked. She had one friend at school who was a fourth grader.

Tracy was an only child and had a fine relationship with her parents. She played with two girls in the neighborhood who were third graders.

By the end of fifth grade, Tracy was achieving more poorly than she had previously. She was anxious because she didn't know why she was having so much trouble. During the summer her parents had her evaluated by an independent professional. On an intelligence scale, Tracy achieved a Full Scale Score of 84. Her achievement test scores and academic functioning in school were commensurate with her measured IQ.

As much effort as Tracy put out in school, she was unable to compete academically with her intellectually more superior classmates. You can imagine the frustration and discouragement a child feels when his best effort is not good enough to achieve average grade-level work. Without special understanding and support, these children are at risk for emotional disturbances and behavior problems.

What Causes Low IQ?

Focusing on and trying to determine the cause of low IQ is a misplacement of valuable time and energy; time and energy that can be spent in assisting your child to release his power for success. The cause of his condition is history. Whatever may have occurred cannot be undone. Most likely a specific cause cannot be identified. Whereas genetic counseling to determine causes of retardation in a child is of value in protecting future children in a family, causes of low IQ are more difficult to ascertain. You must accept your youngster's condition and work with the physician and other team members to assist him in his educational, social, and emotional development.

Nonetheless, most parents cannot resist the temptation to try to determine what led to their youngster's inability to learn well. Searching for the cause of his condition seems to give some kind of meaning to the difficult situation. In the true slow learner, there are two probable causes for the lowered IQ. The first is medical. A number of possibilities fall into this category. Something during the growth of the fetus in the womb can interfere with the normal development of the brain. The mother's use of drugs, alcohol, and tobacco during pregnancy may affect fetal development. A birth injury, birth trauma, or oxygen deprivation during or shortly after birth can result in the disability. An accident causing severe head injury or any process that deprives the brain of oxygen, glucose, or adequate blood flow can contribute to slow learning. Congenital metabolic problems, usually detected during the neonatal screening, are frequently associated with decreased intellectual capacity.

The second cause of low intelligence is genetic. That is, the disorder is inherited. Many slow learners come from families in which other family members have also experienced difficulty learning.

In discussing causes of slow learning, it is important to look at children who appear to be slow learners but who are not. Some children from minority groups, children who use English as a second language, children who are culturally disadvantaged, children who are economically disadvantaged, and children who are severely learning-disabled can encounter enormous difficulty competing in the regular classroom. They can mask as slow learners. Traditional uses of an intelligence scale may even reveal depressed IQ scores for these youngsters.

> Cindy was 11 years old. Her parents had been migrant workers who were rarely in one place for long. Since kindergarten, her school attendance had been erratic and her classroom achievement was far below her fifth-grade placement.
> Upon the untimely death of her father, she and her mother settled in a medium-sized rural community. Her school attendance stabilized, and she liked her classes. An interested teacher arranged to have Cindy evaluated to determine if she qualified for special academic help. Although on the administered intelligence scale and achievement tests she scored below average, other diagnostic tools indicated higher learning potential. Her lowered IQ and achievement were the result of cultural factors.

Like Cindy, sometimes children who mask as slow learners score below average on both an intelligence scale and an achievement test, yet other diagnostic data indicate learning potential higher than the IQ and achievement test number scores. Only a meticulously administered and interpreted evaluation can determine whether a child is a true slow learner or whether another cause is at the root of his inability to successfully achieve.

Characteristics of the Slow Learner

The developmental history of the slow learner is rarely unique or disturbing. The child reaches developmental milestones such as walking and talking within the expected time range. As a preschooler, he may learn more slowly than some children but not enough so to cause concern. It is during kindergarten and the primary grades that the parents of slow learners begin to suspect something is inhibiting their child's learning.

Their youngster has difficulty learning both reading and number concepts. Often the teacher suggests taking a "wait and see" approach with these children when the parents confront her with the problem. This is not always inappropriate. Children mature at different rates and are ready to learn at different times. The young slow learner tends to appear immature and not quite ready to learn.

By the time the youngster reaches third or fourth grade, both his parents and his teachers are sure there is something causing his learning problem. He struggles with all academic subjects and the learning gap between him and his peers widens. Frequently, the child's self-esteem is suffering, he experiences negative feelings about school, and he is unmotivated to involve himself in extracurricular activities.

> Toby was a 10-year-old fourth grader. He was a handsome, polite, soft-spoken boy. His mother requested an evaluation for him because he was receiving C-'s and Ds in all academic subjects. "He studies hard," she said at the parent interview. "He behaves in class and tries hard. He just doesn't seem to be able to catch on."
>
> A review of Toby's birth, babyhood, and early childhood revealed no significant problems. He repeated kindergarten because of immaturity. "Toby is a wonderful little boy who needs some extra time to catch up," was the teacher's comment on the kindergarten report card.
>
> In the primary grades Toby struggled with reading, math, and spelling. His mother had him tutored twice a week to help him "keep up."
>
> During fourth grade, Toby began feeling sick before bedtime most Sunday nights. He resisted going to school Monday mornings and began concealing his homework.

Toby's evaluation resulted in a diagnosis of low average intellectual functioning. He achieved a Full Scale IQ of 80 on the administered intelligence scale and scored below average on each subtest. His achievement test indicated below-grade-level work in all academic subjects. His skills corresponded to his mental ability. Toby's history and testing profile are similar to those of most slow learners. Unlike Toby, many slow-learning youngsters exhibit behavior problems or more severe emotional disturbances than his by the time they reach the middle grades.

The slow learner cannot be picked out of a group of children by his looks, his behavior, or his social skills. His height and weight are consistent with other children of his chronological age. His motor skills are also comparable to his same-age peers. His gross-motor abilities on the playground or athletic field, as well as his small-muscle control, used in cutting or writing, are well-developed for his age. Although the slow-learning child or adolescent may be somewhat delayed socially, it is rarely to a degree that is blatantly apparent. Most slow learners are no more than six months to a year less socially mature than their peers. During adolescence, these youth may be more street-wise than their intellectually brighter counterparts; however, they often fail to use careful judgment and make wise choices.

It is in his ability to comprehend and reason that the slow learner's lower intellectual capacity becomes apparent and where he differs most markedly from his peers. He thinks at a more concrete level than the average child, he takes longer to learn the same material, and he does not remember learned material as well.

On an intelligence scale, slow learners achieve a Full Scale IQ that is below average. Some subtest scores may be within the average range while others may fall quite below. Most will be within one to two years below average for his chronological age. Performance tasks are more apt to yield higher scores than verbal tasks. Scores on achievement tests will probably all fall below grade level. They will usually be consistent with the Full Scale IQ.

In the classroom, the slow learner can be expected to achieve academically between one and two years below grade level. A younger child's achievement will be less delayed than an older child's. The slow learner who has been able to keep pace through the primary grades often begins to experience difficulty by fourth grade. During the middle grades, academic material becomes less concrete. Answers for class discussions, homework, and tests can no longer always be found by locating the right words from the page in a book. The ability to reason, to think through, and to arrive at an answer that is not directly stated is necessary. This ability to think abstractly is not strong in the slow learner.

Schools rarely provide special services for the slow-learning child. He is in a gray area intellectually and educationally. He is not mentally retarded, so he does not qualify for special education. Neither is he able to receive full benefit from regular classroom instruction because the material is too difficult and the competition too great.

You can imagine the stress the child suffers. No matter how hard he tries, he cannot achieve as well as his classmates. The older the child, the greater the educational gap. Keeping the slow learner interested in school and motivated to learn is a difficult task. Providing opportunities for success so that he feels good about himself and his ability to be effective in his life is often a greater challenge.

Remediation for the Slow Learner

It is disturbing and discouraging to parents when the evaluation results indicate their child is a slow learner. Some parents feel a sense of loss and go through a period of grieving. This is a normal reaction. Their loss is compounded when they are told their youngster will not receive services through the school to help him academically. If your child is a slow learner, assistance is available for him outside the school system, and the professional who performed the evaluation will aid you in finding the resources your family needs.

There is no cure for the slow learner; however, academic programs can be modified to meet his needs, and he can learn compensatory skills which will assist him in achieving more successfully.

Academic Remediation

You now well recognize the predicament of the slow learner in the regular classroom. He simply cannot successfully accomplish the curriculum developed for his chronological age group. Within the existing classroom structure, there are a number of possibilities for assisting the student. Modifying the curriculum and the expectations for the learner is mandatory.

> Matt was a tenth-grader in a parochial school.
> The semester project in his history class was to write a
> 20-page term paper on a historical event and to use
> at least 10 sources. The paper was to include foot-
> notes and a bibliography. It was not to summarize
> or tell about the topic, but to evaluate what factors
> in society led to the event and how the event influenced
> subsequent history.
>
> Matt read at an upper-sixth-grade level, and his writing
> skills were at the high-fifth-grade level. Intellectually he
> fell in the low average area of functioning. He did not
> understand the assignment and was overwhelmed with
> the required process.
>
> Matt, his parents, the educational therapist who
> worked with him twice a week, and the classroom
> teacher conferred. The assignment was modified to
> provide the opportunity for his success. He was to use
> three sources and write a six-page paper which
> described what led up to the historical event and the
> event itself. A bibliography was to be included.
>
> Matt accomplished the task and achieved a B grade.

You may have some concern that Matt earned a B on his paper but did not do the tenth-grade assignment. That is an argument that is most frequently raised when discussing curriculum modification for students. This problem is easily handled. When the curriculum is modified for the slow learner, it must be understood by the student and parents that the achieved grades are based on work geared to the student's abilities and not on grade-level work. The student's report card is coded, or an annotation is made in his cumulative record, to explain what his grades reflect.

Ability grouping, often called tracking, is a commonly used technique for meeting individual academic needs. Most middle schools and junior and senior high schools have a tracking system. This means that for many classes the students are grouped according to their intellectual and achievement abilities. Schools have as many as five or more tracks. Track labels differ among school districts. Essentially, tracks are provided for the gifted and talented, college preparatory, average, slow learner, and special education students. Physical education, electives, and some general education classes are not usually tracked. Classes are coded on the report card so that it is understood what achievement level the grades reflect.

Elementary schools rarely track students; however, most classroom teachers use ability grouping for academic subjects. The groups are named by color, number, or original student-chosen titles. Reference is not overtly made to whether a student is in the high, medium, or low group. You can be sure, however, the children are very much aware of where they and their classmates fit into the academic structure.

Grouping and tracking are expedient and efficient ways of meeting students' needs. Within ability groups, individualizing of assignments is necessary for some students. The assumption is made that most students can achieve at the group level. For the student who cannot, individualizing his assignments is imperative for his success.

Tutoring is necessary for the success of slow learners once they are beyond the primary grades. As classroom assignments become more complex and as homework increases, the students need assistance in both comprehending and keeping up with the work. A number of options are available.

Peer tutoring is help given by one student to another.

> Robert, an eighth grader, did not read well. He could
> sound out words but did not comprehend what he read.
> To aid him with his classwork, he was assigned a peer tutor.
> During part of each day, Randy, also an eighth grader,
> worked with Robert. He read the history assignments
> to him and helped him with answering questions or
> doing worksheets. He did not do Robert's worksheets
> for him but served as a support and assistant.

Peer tutors serve a vital purpose for the slow learner. As well as academic help, they provide support different from that found between a child or adolescent and an adult. Sometimes they can get a concept across through their choice of words and examples that an adult cannot.

College-bound high school students often are available to tutor both their peers and younger students. The fee they charge for their services is lower than that received by adult tutors and educational therapists. Local high schools keep updated lists of qualified students who are available for tutoring. You can call the high school nearest you for available students. Making the tutoring arrangements is your responsibility. The school does not participate in that process. When peer tutors or high school students are used, it is important to make sure your child is being assisted with his work and not having the assignments done for him.

The current emphasis on underachievement and learning problems has led to an abundance of centers developed to bolster the skills of the child with academic difficulties. Some remediate a single skill such as reading. Others work with all academic subject matter. When a student enrolls in a learning center, diagnostic work is done and a learning program developed. The student generally attends the center from one to three hours a week. Most communities have at least one learning center, and larger communities have several. Study skills classes are offered through local park and recreation programs and through community college programs developed for school-age children and youth. Some libraries have learning assistance as part of their program. To find programs in your area, look under "Schools" in the yellow pages of your phone directory. A guide to finding specific services is provided. Also, your child's school can tell you the available resources in your community.

The quality of tutoring varies markedly among learning-assistance programs. Some programs use only credentialed teachers, some have their own staff training, and others require their tutors to have little more than a desire to work with people. Before enrolling your child in a learning center, ask about the qualifications of the staff, what services are available, and what fees are charged. Once you enroll him, keep abreast of his progress through periodic conferences. It is your right and responsibility to know how your child is progressing.

A final form of educational intervention is the independent tutor and educational therapist. Tutors generally charge a lower hourly fee than educational therapists, and they may or may not have specialized training. They frequently are or have been classroom teachers or are college students. Educational therapists have master's or doctor's degrees and are trained in educating the student with learning problems.

When you are looking for a tutor, check with the local school district or university. They often keep lists of available tutors. Sometimes tutors advertise in local newspapers. Your pediatrician, the person who evaluated your child, or the local school can give you the names of educational therapists. When seeking the services of private professionals, be aware of the person's training, the fees they charge, and what services they offer. Periodic parent conferences are a necessary aspect of private help. If they are not regularly scheduled by the professional, request them. As a parent, you have the power and right to request what you are not receiving.

The goal of tutoring for the slow learner is not necessarily to increase his academic skills, although for some this may be an essential part of the program. For many of these youth, academic assistance needs to be viewed as a way of helping them understand the material they are working on and as an aid to staying caught-up with current assignments. Assistance with homework and reinforcement of the skills taught in the classroom are reasonable expectations. Tutoring sessions must include the strengthening or teaching of compensatory skills and the use of compensatory tools which are so necessary to the slow learner's success.

Compensatory skills are techniques that help to offset or counterbalance a deficiency. Compensatory tools are devices that allow for greater efficiency and success. A common compensatory tool used by adults and children alike is the calculator. This instrument cuts down the amount of time spent in figuring answers to mathematical problems. It also allows one to use mathematical functions he may not know how to manually compute. The calculator is a useful tool for the slow learner. It provides the opportunity for him to complete assignments and achieve greater accuracy than he otherwise might. "Shouldn't kids know how to do math?" you wonder. Yes. Children need to learn the basic processes of addition, subtraction, multiplication, and division. More importantly, they need to know when to use the various functions. As adults in the working world, however, they will seldom be called upon to use the skills without the aid of a mechanical device. Learning how to use such machines provides the opportunity for greater academic success during the school years. Computers, tape recorders, and typewriters are other tools the slow learner can effectively learn to use. These machines diminish the amount of time it takes to complete assignments, can work as incentives to do the assignments, and lead to greater accuracy in classwork and homework.

Compensatory skills include tasks such as learning how to write down assignments, how to correctly head papers, how to organize notebooks, and how to study for tests. Being an effective student depends on these essential skills. How to find the needed information on a page which answers comprehension questions, and how to answer the questions with only the necessary information are two skills that need to be taught. These kinds of issues must be addressed by both the classroom teacher and the tutor or educational therapist if the slow learner is to achieve maximum success.

The school program for the slow learner is most effective if it is practically oriented. It must provide tasks which allow him to succeed as a student and later in the working world. Basic academics, consumer skills, vocational training, and on-the-job experience are mandatory. Opportunities to learn leisure-time activities and to practice effective decision making need to be incorporated into the learning program. Experiencing success in as many and varied ways as imaginative educators can create is the surest path to successful adulthood for the slow learner.

Support in the Home

Your job in parenting your slow-learning offspring cannot be overestimated. Both your understanding of his struggles and your acceptance of him pave the way for self-acceptance and success.

It is hard to be patient when a child does not live up to your expectations. Developing patience is a necessary asset in parenting the slow learner. He needs your support and encouragement. He needs to know that you have faith and trust in him regardless of his learning abilities. Accepting and expecting his best efforts, without pushing for achievement beyond his abilities, indicate your respect for him. The slow learner takes longer to complete academic work than his peers and siblings. Allow the extra time for him to complete his homework and encourage his efforts. Assist him with his homework when necessary without taking over the task. Remember, his best is not your best.

Effective parenting requires recognizing your youngster's strengths and helping him build on them without being overly protective.

> Josh loved animals. As a child, he lived in an apartment which did not allow pets.
>
> When he was seven, he and his mother talked to the owner of a local pet shop, and Josh was invited to help feed the animals each afternoon.
>
> During junior high school, Josh placed a notice on the local market bulletin board stating that he would feed and walk neighborhood pets while owners were on vacation. He earned spending money while doing this, as well as fulfilling his desire to be with animals.
>
> As a high school student, Josh worked weekends and summers in a pet shop. His experiences gave him the opportunity to learn responsibility, to work effectively with people, and to increase his skills in caring for animals.

It may take some real detective work to discover what your child is deeply interested in and how it can be tapped. Resourceful parents can help their children develop their skills and talents in unusual and creative ways.

As your child grows older, he needs your continued support, although he will probably not want you integrally involved in his learning process. It is important for you to be available to discuss school, friendships, or other aspects of his life without insisting on such sharing. This keeps the doors of communication open. Recognizing academic and social success and showing appreciation for good judgment and careful choices helps him to be aware of his appropriate behaviors. Exploring academic and career options together assists your son or daughter in decision making.

Your effective parenting is the most valuable of all tools in fostering your youngster's emotional growth and success. Learn the skills and use them consistently. Keep in mind that he is more like other children than he is different from them. He wants to succeed and achieve, and he needs your faith and support to do so. He needs your guidance to work through the feelings of frustration and worthlessness he experiences as a result of regularly being confronted with tasks that are too hard for him. There may be times when he needs the assistance of a mental health therapist to work on emotional or behavioral problems. Providing this experience for him is an indication of your loving support.

What About the Future?

While your child is in school, the school counselors will assist in appropriate class placement. In most high schools, during the junior and senior years, career or vocational testing and counseling are available. The information gained assists teenagers in making decisions regarding post-high-school education or employment. If this service is not provided in your youngster's high school, a few sessions with a private career counselor can be a worthwhile investment in his future. Participation in the Regional Occupation Program, ROP, is available for individuals 16 years of age and older and provides on-the-job training for those who use this service.

Some doors will not be open to the slow learner in higher education and careers; however, there are post-high-school educational opportunities at community colleges and vocational schools as well as on-the-job training. To expect that your child will become a doctor, lawyer, or teacher is not reasonable. To know that he has the potential for responsible employment in worthwhile jobs is realistic and appropriate.

An important point to remember is that the diagnosis of slow learner is school-related. The problems experienced by these youth are essentially academic. If the condition is diagnosed early and appropriate intervention is employed, slow learners do not become socially and emotionally impaired. They release their power for success and live successful and satisfying adult lives.

Check List for the Slow Learner

The following check list includes many of the characteristics common to the slow learner. Although it is not all-inclusive, it does cover those most frequently seen. There are 26 response possibilities on the list. If you answer "Yes" on at least 20 of the items, and numbers 8 to 12 are "Yes," your youngster's learning problems could be because he is a slow learner. Discuss your concerns with your pediatrician and school counselor or administrator. You may want to take this list with you.

	Yes	No
1. My child reached early developmental milestones within the normal time range: a. Crawling		
b. Walking		
c. Talking		
d. Toilet training		
2. My child falls within the normal range in height.		
3. My child falls within the normal range in weight.		
4. My child performs the following gross-motor tasks as well as other children his age: a. Walking		
b. Running		
c. Skipping		
d. Jumping		
e. Hopping on one foot		
f. Throwing a ball		
g. Catching a ball		
5. My child performs the following fine-motor tasks as well as other children his age: a. Picking up small objects with thumb and forefinger		

continued . . .

	Yes	No
b. Cutting with scissors		
c. Coloring within lines		
d. Printing or writing		
6. My child has at least two friends.		
7. My child is not quite as mature socially as other children his age.		
8. My child does not seem to learn as quickly as other children his age.		
9. My child reads below grade level.		
10. My child's math skills are below grade level.		
11. My child's spelling skills are below grade level.		
12 My child's citizenship grades are usually satisfactory.		
13. My child's effort grades are usually satisfactory.		

Check List for Evaluation of Services

The following check list will help you evaluate the services your child is receiving if he has already been diagnosed as a slow learner. If he is not receiving the assistance he needs to release his power for success, speak to the classroom teacher or educational therapist working with him. You may want to take this list with you.

	Yes	No
1. After the diagnosis, my child's disability was explained to me in terms I understood.		
2. Methods for assisting my child were presented to me.		
3. My child's disability was explained to him in appropriate terms.		
4. My child was told how he could be helped.		
5. My child's responsibility in the remediation process was explained to him.		
6. The classroom teacher individualizes my child's program through: a. Modification of assignments		
b. Academic grouping by ability		
c. Peer tutoring		
d. Teaching compensatory skills		
7. The private tutor assists my child by: a. Helping him understand homework assignments		
b. Providing tasks which reinforce skills similar to those he learns in school		
c. Teaching compensatory skills		

11

The Power of Success

In our society we have an educational problem of serious magnitude. This problem is so large that it affects millions of school-age children. Until recently, we have called this problem underachievement. We now know better. Underachievement is not the problem. It is a result of the problem. Underachievement is the result of something that prohibits a child from learning effectively. To solve the problem, we must discover what that something is and treat it, so that the child can release his power for success.

From your reading of the first 10 chapters, you know that guiding your youngster toward success requires 10 steps:

1. Recognize that a problem exists
2. Discuss your concerns with your child's physician
3. Have the appropriate evaluations
4. Follow through with the recommendations provided
5. Be an effective consumer of professional services
6. Ask for what you are not getting
7. Increase your repertoire of parenting skills
8. Use your parenting skills consistently
9. Create experiences where your child can succeed
10. Acknowledge each step toward success

None of these steps reveals a deep secret. None is new or earthshattering. Each is something you have probably heard before. What makes our method work is the systematic following of each step and the use of a team approach with the child. The team is composed of the child, parent, physician, learning specialist, mental health worker, and classroom teacher.

This concept of using a team is not newer than any of the 10 steps of our system. Multidisciplinary teams have been used for years in public schools and in the private sector. What contributes to the uniqueness and workability of the team approach we use, is the ongoing commitment and communication among team members during the child's entire evaluation and treatment process. In each step of his journey toward success, the professionals encourage parent involvement and maintain contact with each other.

Let us review the 10 steps, note which team members are involved in each step, and summarize the ways in which they work with you, the child, and each other.

1. *Recognize that a problem exists.* It is not easy to admit that your youngster is having problems. Once you acknowledge the situation, you either have to do something about it or hope that it will go away. Most problems do not go away by themselves. The symptoms of underachievement never do. The longer the underachiever remains undiagnosed, the greater the academic, social, and emotional problems he faces. Sometimes you are the first person to notice behaviors in your youngster that signal all is not well with him academically. Sometimes the classroom teacher alerts you. In either case, be a loving and effective parent and take the next step.

2. *Discuss your concerns with the child's physician.* Use the check list at the end of chapter 2. It will help you clarify how your youngster is currently functioning. Take notes about the concerns his classroom teacher has. Formulate questions you have. Make your time with the physician count. He will probably provide as much time as you need, but he can best assist you when you are prepared. Doctors who work with children know developmental patterns. Your physician can deny or confirm a possible problem. When he believes a problem exists, he guides you toward the next step.

3. *Have the appropriate evaluations.* A medical evaluation is a wise place to begin. During the evaluation, the physician takes a medical history. You provide most of the pertinent information in this valuable process. The history provides the leads to the cause of underachievement. After the medical history, your youngster has a physical examination. When necessary, laboratory tests are prescribed. The medical evaluation either confirms or rules out medical causes for the underachievement.

Next an educational-psychological evaluation is undertaken. It can be done through the school district or privately. This evaluation reveals intellectual and emotional processes which interfere with learning and sheds light on how identified physical disorders create blocks to achievement. An educational therapist, mental health professional, or both participate in this step.

The medical and educational-psychological evaluations result in a diagnosis. Diagnoses which contribute to underachievement are attention deficit disorder with and without hyperactivity, learning disability, emotional disorders, low IQ, and certain medical problems.

4. *Follow through with the recommendations provided.* Both the physician and the professional who administers the educational-psychological evaluation provide you with recommendations for assisting your child toward achievement. Follow them! An evaluation is a waste of your child's time and of your time and money if you do not. An evaluation clarifies what the problem is, and it provides the information necessary in setting up an effective treatment program. It does not solve the problem. Only following the recommended treatment steps does that. Each member of the team plays a role in this step.

5. *Be an effective consumer of professional services.* Through reading this book, you have learned what to expect from the professionals who work with your child. You know what constitutes an effective remediation and treatment program. Reread any material which is pertinent to your particular situation. Use the check lists at the ends of the chapters. The information can help you verbalize questions you have about your youngster's treatment. Professionals appreciate parents who honestly and straightforwardly express concerns or provide new information.

6. *Ask for what you are not getting.* It is your responsibility and right to make sure your youngster is receiving effective remediation and treatment. The Check List for Evaluation of Services at the end of each chapter summarizes the important parts of an effective treatment program. If you do not feel you are receiving these services, talk to the professional working with your family. You may even want to take the check list with you. The professional can take this opportunity to clarify the treatment process with you. Any reputable professional gladly does this.

7. *Increase your repertoire of parenting skills.* Effective parenting of an underachieving child is challenging. We recognize this challenge and in each chapter have provided effective-parenting techniques which, when lovingly and consistently used, effect change in your youngster's behavior. There are many excellent parenting books on the market for you to choose from if you want further information. The physician and other professionals working with you often offer suggestions suited to your particular family. The time you take to learn and practice effective parenting pays enormous dividends. When you and your offspring communicate openly with each other and trust each other, the security he feels provides the base for increased academic and social success. Effective parenting does not happen overnight. Be patient with yourself and resist thinking a technique does not work until you have really given it your best effort. Progress takes time.

8. *Use your parenting skills consistently.* No one is 100 percent consistent at anything. In effectively parenting your underachieving child, aim for the 100 percent mark, and you will hit about 80 percent. That is terrific. When your youngster knows what to expect, he responds positively, both to the standards in your home which you and he have developed and to your loving guidance. When he knows that you mean what you say and are willing to follow through on that, he feels more secure. A secure child is a successful child.

9. *Create experiences where your child can succeed.* Loving your underachieving child must include more than feelings of affection. You must also create an environment in which he experiences success. Underachievers do not do well at creating success for themselves. They need to have structured experiences which ensure likely success until they begin to see themselves as capable. Structure in the home and school, clearly stated standards with built-in consequences, consistency, open communication, and plenty of encouragement create an environment where they can release their power for success.

10. *Acknowledge each step toward success.* Remember how excited you were when your youngster started walking? Each tiny step he took was a time for rejoicing. When he took two steps, then plopped down on his little bottom, you encouraged him to stand up and try again. He needs that same enthusiasm and encouragement from you now. Each step he takes

away from underachievement and toward success feels precarious to him. He is not on sure ground. He needs to know that you care and support him in his journey. Do not expect perfection; growth is always a process of two steps forward and one step back. Recognize his partial success by encouraging any positive behavior you see. Success is built with success. Help your child recognize the progress he is making regardless of how large or small. Appreciate his efforts. He wants to succeed, and he wants you to know it!

Your child is unique. There has never been anyone nor will there ever be anyone quite like him. His path toward success is not the same as any other underachiever's. At the same time that your youngster is unique, he is also very much like everyone else, including other underachievers. It is because of this fact alone that we know, without doubt, if you follow the 10 steps, he cannot help releasing his power for success. Hundreds of underachieving children have. So can he!

I've Done This Before

"I hear what you're saying, but we've tried all this before, and it hasn't worked," say some parents when we present our 10-step plan to them. It seems probable that whatever has been tried has not been done in the way we are suggesting. We know that many, many underachieving children have not moved into success with the professional help they have received. That is because there has been a breakdown of some sort at some point along the way. If you have had intervention in the past that has not worked, you are probably reluctant to try again. Let us look at some of the breakdowns that might have prohibited success from occurring.

1. *The evaluation was not complete.* The only way to successfully determine what is causing your youngster's underachievement is to have a medical and educational-psychological evaluation. If one or the other is ignored or is incomplete, adequate information for developing effective treatment is not available.

2. *The evaluation results were inconclusive.* This is very frustrating. After you have spent the time and money for an evaluation, you expect an answer to your youngster's problem. To be told, "Yes, Zach does have a

problem, but it is unclear as to why he is achieving as poorly as he is," is not satisfactory. Sometimes initial results are inconclusive. When a child is very young this is especially true. In children of any age, one disorder may mask as another. Nonetheless, an evaluator who knows her business well knows the tools to use to clarify the primary problem. She becomes an explorer and carefully works with your child until she discovers what is interfering with his ability to achieve.

3. *Sufficient recommendations were not made.* There are evaluators who can determine what a problem is, but who are not effective at using the information to develop a successful treatment plan. Without a clear series of steps to take to assist the underachiever, he does not improve.

4. *Remediation did not meet your child's needs.* All disorders leading to underachievement have an emotional component. If the intervention did not address both the educational and emotional aspects of your child's disorder, only partial results could be expected. Not all therapists can assist with both educational and emotional problems. It may be necessary to have two individuals work with your child for optimal results. If the educational remediation was not tailored to your youngster's unique needs, success could not occur.

5. *You did not follow through on the home front.* If you lost hope and gave up following the recommendations for use at home, your child was not receiving the opportunity to become an achiever. What goes on in the home cannot be over-emphasized. One hour of educational or psychological therapy each week is not likely to result in major behavior change in your youngster. Your guidance and effective parenting are necessary for his success.

6. *The school did not follow through.* The classroom teacher is an integral part of the therapeutic team. Individualizing of the underachiever's academic program, structure in the classroom, and consistency in maintaining classroom standards is necessary for your youngster's optimal growth.

After these reasons for previous lack of growth toward success have been explored, some parents say, "Well, I think everyone has done all they can do. Jennifer just refuses to respond. I think she just doesn't care." Of course she cares. Everyone wants to be successful. In cases like Jennifer's, it is important to examine how her success at underachieving serves her so well that moving into achievement does not seem worth the risks or effort. This becomes an important issue in effective psychological treatment. On the other hand, maybe Jennifer's parents and the significant others in her life were unable to recognize her small successes. Severely disordered children and children who lack strong motivation can appear to make little or no progress. No child is totally ineffective. It takes a trained eye to see small increments of growth and success. Throughout the previous pages, we have provided information to raise your awareness of the kinds of growth to look for. Your positive recognition and acknowledgment of even the smallest appropriate behavior are imperative for your youngster's continued growth.

Ultimately, of course, the underachiever's success is up to him. No one can be successful for him. In order to release his power for success, he must be responsive to the interventions used. If the therapeutic team works together and each member is consistent with him, lack of response is virtually impossible. It takes commitment on the part of each team member for the underachiever to grow into a successful student. Pediatricians, teachers, educational and mental health therapists work with children because they want to. They want to see children succeed in their lives. They are very willing to work with each other and the parent to assist a youngster in releasing his power for success. Commitment to the 10-step program on the part of each team member results in the success that is a joy to the child and everyone involved with him.

Let Me Think About It

Sometimes, after the completion of the medical evaluation and the recommendation for an educational-psychological evaluation has been made, a parent says, "I know Brent needs help, and I don't want him to get farther behind, but let me think about it."

The commitment to assisting your youngster in releasing his power for success is not easy. It necessitates time, effort, patience, and money. Your time is at a premium. When you work all day, you want your non-work time to be hassle-free. You do not want to make commitments that interfere with that time. We understand that. We also know you believe that it is your responsibility to parent as effectively as possible. That can mean spending the time necessary to help your youngster move from underachievement to success. Effort and patience are not easy qualities to express when you are tired from work and frustrated with parenting your underachiever. They are essential to his success, however, and are qualities that you can develop. For your peace of mind, for the effective functioning of your family, and for the success of your underachieving child, it is worth the effort it takes to develop them. It is easier to put effort into your parenting and to be patient with your youngster when you understand his problem. From reading this book, you have gained knowledge and understanding which help you feel empathy for him. This results in greater patience.

The issue of cost is foremost in the minds of many parents. They want to provide the best for their youngster, but do not feel they can afford to. Assisting an underachiever toward success is costly. In the long run, it is far more costly to let him flounder. The toll an unsuccessful child takes on himself, his family, and on society cannot be measured. In the short run, however, a family's financial position must play a role in the steps they choose to take.

When you believe you cannot afford the services to assist your youngster, there are some avenues to consider before you make your final decision. If you have medical insurance, it covers a portion of the medical evaluation. If your policy includes coverage for mental health services, it may pay part of the educational-psychological evaluation and follow-up treatment. There are differences among insurance companies and between states on mental health coverage. Insurance does not cover the fees of an educational therapist or tutor. Some professionals provide service on a sliding fee scale. That is, their fee is charged according to your income. Almost all professionals are willing to work out a payment plan with you. As long as you are able to pay a portion of the charge for each visit or a percentage of your monthly bill, they do not deny you the assistance you need. Also, remember that educational-psychological evaluations are available through your school district for many children. They are provided free of charge. Review chapter 3 for information about this. When you are committed to assisting your child in releasing his power for success, it can be done.

I Really Want To, and I Just Can't

You requested an educational-psychological evaluation from the school district and were denied. You talked to your pediatrician and an educational or mental health professional and were unable to work out an adequate financial arrangement. You reviewed your priorities and simply cannot follow each of the steps in the 10-step program we recommend. Does your youngster need to stay stuck in underachievement? Absolutely not! There are steps you can take which cost absolutely nothing. Discuss your youngster's problem with his classroom teacher, and ask her to individualize his academic program, if she is not already doing so. Check out the possibility of peer tutoring during the day with a classmate. Increase your parenting skills. By simply reading the sections devoted to parenting in each chapter of this book, you can learn new ways to interact with your youngster. Read some of the excellent parenting books on the market that are devoted entirely to issues of parenting. For a small fee, you can enroll in a parent education class offered through your local community college or community services and recreation department. Group support is extremely valuable when you are working on change.

We cannot tell you how much progress your youngster will make if you use only these steps. We do know that he will grow into greater success than he is currently experiencing. All of us respond to loving guidance and effective communication. Your child is no different. Whatever commitment you can make to his increased achievement, if it is done lovingly, honestly, and consistently, he will respond.

The Power of Success

Everyone has the capacity for success, and everyone wants to be successful. It is an inherent part of our nature. It is such a driving force in our lives that, when we cannot succeed in positive ways, we develop negative behavior patterns and become successful at those. Underachievers become successful at not succeeding. Lasting rewards for their negative success are few.

The underachiever can succeed. He has proven that. He wants to succeed in a way that is acceptable to you and society, and he does not know how. With your assistance, he can learn how. You now know that there are ways to unlock the capabilities that lie beneath his inability to learn effectively.

When you give your underachieving child the opportunity to experience the power of success, he delights in himself and his achievement, and you experience the joy of parenting a happy, successful child.

Index

Order Form

Please send me _____ copy(ies) of *Underachievement: Reversing the Process* (ISBN 0-9628925-1-3).

Price (# of books x $13.95)_____
CA Residents add 6.5% tax_____
Shipping and handling
$2.00, first book–each
additional book $1.00   _____
Total $_____

❑ I enclose check or money order made payable to Family Life Publications.
❑ Please charge my ❑ Visa ❑ Mastercard
Card #_____Expiration date_____
Signature_____

Name_____

Address_____

_____

Phone (   )_____

Please allow three to four weeks for delivery.

Send to: Family Life Publications
P. O. Box 1589
Sunset Beach, California 90742-1589

Sunset Beach, California